T.. Grand Union Canal

(North)

Nick Corble

TEMPUS

OTHER BOOKS IN THE TOWPATH SERIES:

The Grand Union Canal (South)
The Kennet & Avon
The South Oxford Canal

First published 2006

Tempus Publishing Limited
The Mill, Brimscombe Port,
Stroud, Gloucestershire, GL5 2QG

© Nick Corble, 2006

The right of Nick Corble to be identified as the Author
of this work has been asserted in accordance with the
Copyrights, Designs and Patents Act 1988.

British Library Cataloguing in Publication Data.
A catalogue record for this book is available from the British Library.

ISBN 0 7524 3803 4

Typesetting and design by Liz Rudderham
Origination by Tempus Publishing Limited
Printed and bound in Great Britain

CONTENTS

INTRODUCTION

The renaissance of the canals towards the latter end of the last century was one of the country's greatest, but largely unsung, success stories. A major new leisure resource emerged that somehow managed to bring together our collective love of the countryside, our pride in our past and our growing need for an escape from the fast pace of modern living. There is no doubt about it; the canals, once in danger of being filled in and erased from history, are here to stay.

Perhaps the most distinguishing feature of our canal system is the boats that ply their way slowly but steadily through it. However, although boaters clearly represent the most visible group of canal users, they are by no means the only ones to appreciate their worth. It has been estimated that over 400 million visits are made to the canal system each year, only 2 million of which are by boaters.

The reality is that the canals have become more than simply a transport system; they have evolved into visitor corridors. Walkers, riders, anglers, cyclists or simply those among the half of the population who live within 5 miles of an inland waterway now regularly pass through these corridors. Cyclists alone account for three times as many visits as boaters and the total number expected to utilise the canals is expected to double over the coming decade.

These new Guides have been written to reflect this burgeoning reality. They have been written to appeal to boaters but to reach out beyond them to these other groups – the backpacker planning a towpath walk, motorists looking to spend a long weekend staying in bed and breakfasts, riders looking to discover the joy of towpath routes... the list goes on.

The Guides have been prepared to inform, amuse and spark an interest in the areas surrounding the canals, with the visitor corridor being defined as spanning 2 miles either side of the towpath. Anecdotes and interesting facts are scattered throughout the Guides to provide colour and bring these areas alive to the reader, with only the most resilient likely to resist the temptation to repeat at least some of these to their companions.

For ease of use, each canal is broken down into sections covering between 7-13 miles, with sections themselves broken down into the following four groupings:

SHAPERS
Describing the route of the canal, the local history associated with it and details of the natural landscape and transport links, this section provides the basic background to each section.

BASICS
Where to shop, find a pub or locate a place to stay as well as places to eat. All these topics are covered under this heading, taking the sting out of finding your way around and the essentials of getting by.

SEEING AND DOING

What to look out for and where it's worth making a diversion to see that oddity or curiosity you might not otherwise find, plus where to find that something a bit special culturally or where to go if you simply want to be entertained.

SAMPLING

Ways to dip into the local area and become part of the landscape, whether you are walking or cycling (a recommended route is provided for both in each section), riding, fishing or want to wander around a golf course.

Each section is accompanied by maps complete with symbols to show you where to find places highlighted in the text, with larger symbols indicating a concentration of pubs, hotels etc. Phone numbers and websites are given as appropriate and the 'Learn More and Links' section provides pointers on where to look if you want to follow up on items covered in the Guide – making it simple if you want to check a pub's opening hours, whether a leisure centre has a squash court or the times of a local bus.

   We hope that these new Guides will encourage more people to enjoy our inland waterways and help them to deepen their appreciation of the symbiotic relationship between the canals and the towns and villages that surround them.

Nick Corble
Series Editor

NOTE: *Cyclists need a permit from British Waterways – either apply direct or download one from their website www.britishwaterways.co.uk. Likewise, anglers should check who controls fishing rights on particular stretches and details are provided in this Guide.*

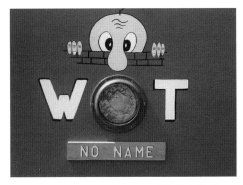

What's in a name?

OVERVIEW

The Grand Union Canal is the 'M1' of the canal system, linking as it does the country's capital with its 'second city'.

This Guide covers the northern half of the canal, starting just north of Birmingham and passes through Warwick and Leamington Spa before cruising through the flatlands of Northamptonshire and ending just north of Milton Keynes, among the small villages and towns now absorbed into that city's shadow.

While Birmingham is covered in depth in this Guide, Milton Keynes is featured in the sister volume in this series, *The Grand Union Canal (South),* also available from Tempus Publishing.

Today, this route is a favourite for the modern leisure boater, but it was originally built to serve a very different purpose. By the end of the eighteenth century the coalfields of the Midlands needed to get their black gold to markets in the south and the natural advantages of water transport for bulk freight were well understood. After considerable struggle a canal had been cut from Coventry to Oxford, and thence via the Thames to London, its first cargo of coal arriving in the university city in 1790.

Although effective, the Oxford route was less than efficient, its route following a tortuous and meandering course. Furthermore, Oxford still sat some way up the Thames, a less than easy waterway to negotiate with boaters having to 'ride' weirs rather than use locks to manage the slope down to sea level.

There was scope for an alternative. An Act of Parliament in 1793 authorised the construction of a canal from Braunston in Northamptonshire down to Brentford, with the new waterway to be called the Grand Junction.

From Braunston it was possible to link up with the Warwick and Napton and the Warwick and Birmingham Canals, and thence into the heart of Birmingham itself. This was a much more direct route than that provided by the Coventry and Oxford Canals, especially considering this required using the Birmingham and Fazeley Canal which necessitated going north before heading south.

> The Grand Junction Canal was one of the main transport arteries of Georgian England, carrying the supplies for Nelson's ships and Wellington's army, and allowing the country to pursue its war against Napoleon.

Alternatively, from 1802 boaters had the option of leaving the Warwick and Birmingham Canal at Kingswood Junction and joining the new Stratford Canal, which offered a route into the south of Birmingham.

Although it suffered its ups and downs, the route from Braunston via Warwick began to gain favour over the old route via Oxford. The new canal had the advantage of being both broad and altogether more ambitious. Gone was the adherence to following the contour and in came grand engineering, with long tunnels at Blisworth and Braunston, an aqueduct over the Ouse and a long flight of locks at Hatton.

Unfortunately, the opportunity was not taken to bring the new broad width all the way into Birmingham itself, a decision which would later come back to haunt both the canal and the town. Although this decision was driven by narrow parochial interests, it would not have been surprising if the difficulties the new daring canal engineers were having were also an influence when this decision was made.

The aqueduct over the Ouse, west of what is now Milton Keynes, was particularly troublesome. Not only did the embankment collapse but the brick aqueduct itself fell into the river after only three years, leading to a slight delay while a cast-iron version was built and put in place.

The tunnel at Blisworth was similarly awkward. Two attempts were required as internal flooding and quicksand led to the abandonment of the first, and the canal company proved to be hesitant in its decision making. As time passed, the tunnel proved to be the missing piece in the jigsaw, and it was not until 1805 that a through route from Birmingham to London avoiding the Thames became possible.

After the initial difficulties at Blisworth, the canal's engineer, William Jessop, proposed taking the canal over the top of the hill using a flight of twenty-nine locks. Fortunately, he was overruled by Robert Whitworth and John Rennie, who advocated a new route 130 yards to the west of the original tunnel. This proved to be a success, the total bill for the new tunnel finally coming to £90,000.

Commercial success followed, but it proved to be ephemeral. The railways were coming and in less than thirty years the first main trunk route was, quite understandably, one linking London and Birmingham. With the final portion of the route still narrow rather than broad, the canal's limitations against the speed and efficiency of rail were magnified.

For a long while there was enough trade to keep both routes going, but the canals only survived by paring their costs to a minimum. It is from around this time that bargee wages were slashed to such an extent that they were forced to make homes on their boats alongside their families.

An old Fellows, Morton & Clayton cargo boat.

A Fellows Sears and Morton boat.

Like struggling companies through time, the company had followed a strategy of expansion in a desperate search for growth, and had swallowed up the Leicester Line in 1897. With the Great Depression of the late 1920s, when the Grand Junction joined forces with the Regent's Canal and the canals north and west of Braunston, the Grand Union as we know it today came into being.

Government assistance aimed at creating jobs saw the narrow locks closer to Birmingham widened, and in 1934 the Grand Union Canal Carrying Co., the GUCCC, whose initials are a regular feature along the canal on signs, bridges and boats, was formed.

The large fleet of boats, built especially for the company, came too late. The days of canal freight as a realistic alternative to the roads and railways were over. Nationalisation followed in 1949, and most of the boats carrying the company's insignia were scrapped. However, some still ply the waters today, either restored to their original form or converted to leisure use.

This Guide starts north of Birmingham at the Salford Junction with the Birmingham and Fazeley Canal, avoiding the more glamorous parts of that city's canal network in favour of a more industrial landscape, before finding a rural equilibrium around the intriguingly named canalside village of Catherine de Barnes. A short flight of locks at Knowle proves to be a slight aberration as the towpath remains flat as far as the Shrewley Tunnel, south of the Kingswood Junction with the Stratford Canal and slightly beyond.

It more than makes up for this with the dramatic Hatton Flight, west of Warwick. After a long rural stretch, Warwick and its near neighbour, Leamington Spa, provide a more built-up landscape, although the canal itself manages to avoid the centres of both these towns. Views down onto the Avon from an aqueduct between the two provide a taste for things to come.

Locks at Bascote, including a staircase, as well as the Stockton and Calcutt Flights, bring the canal onto the 5-mile stretch linking this section with the

Grand Junction at Braunston, a run of water that is technically part of the Oxford Canal.

The first of the canal's two long tunnels follows on reaching Braunston, with Braunston Turn to the west marking the beginning of the North Oxford Canal, and Norton Junction to the east, the link with the Leicester Section of the Grand Union. Our route takes us south, through more locks and past the Gaydon Junction with the Northamptonshire Arm of the canal.

The other great tunnel follows, that at Blisworth, with the pretty canal village of Stoke Bruerne waiting on the other side. Another short flight follows, but from here on, the scenery is flat all the way to Cosgrove, where the splendour of the Great Ouse Aqueduct awaits with its magnificent views.

The Guide leaves the towpath traveller in the areas to the north of Milton Keynes, which still cling to some sense of independence, including Stony Stratford and Wolverton. The metropolis of Milton Keynes itself lies to the south, and is more easily reached from the towpath further on.

The section of the Grand Union covered in this Guide has a certain symmetry, with two brash urban centres bookending it and long flat stretches of calm between them, pivoted by the Georgian grandeur of Warwick and Leamington Spa. In between, there is a good variety of rivers, which sometimes provide floodplains for the canal to share, and sometimes offer dramatic valleys and views. Equally, there is no shortage of triumphs of engineering, some obvious, others less visible having blended in to the landscape after 200 years. To top it all, there is the 'jewel in the crown' of Stoke Bruerne, the very epitome of a canal village.

Whether you are walking, cycling or boating down the canal, we hope this Guide will be useful to you – in drawing your attention to things you might otherwise have missed, providing more background to those more obvious of its features and giving you the basic information you need to make your journey more pleasant and stress-free.

Not all boaters are dog-lovers!

SECTION A

SALFORD JUNCTION TO CATHERINE DE BARNES

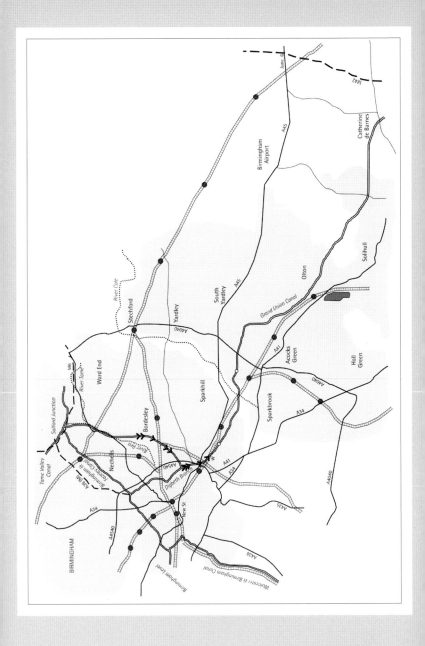

Key

══════	Canal	🔵 Built up area		⭘	Turning point
··········	River	🔴 Stations		⋀	Lock
▦▦▦▦▦	Railway	🔵 Open water		Ⓑ	Boatyard
─ ─ ─	Motorway			W	Waterpoint
─────	A Road				
─────	B Road				

SHAPERS

THE CANAL ON THIS STRETCH

KEY FACTS

LENGTH: 10 miles

BOATYARDS: 1
    Camp Hill

TURNING POINTS: 2
    Camp Hill
    Hay Mills

LOCKS: 11
    Garrison Locks (5) (34ft 5in)
    Camp Hill Locks (6) (41ft 8in)

This is not the prettiest stretch of canal but for purists it has the virtue of offering an example of what an authentic working waterway would have looked like in its heyday, with industrial landscapes very much the theme, at least in the early stages. Locks are concentrated at the start and services are scant, as are moorings. Generally, this is an area to pass through and observe rather than stop, with boaters looking to pause strongly advised to continue into the heart of Birmingham via the Digbeth Branch.

The Grand Union starts unpromisingly at Salford Junction, where it joins the Birmingham and Fazeley Canal under the shadow and noise of the M6 flyover and next to a pair of graffiti-covered bridges. It passes immediately beneath the A47 and over the River Tame, while the distinctive turquoise blue of the StarCity leisure complex soon looms on the left (see Seeing and Doing).

The route along here is uncompromisingly straight and obstacle-free, with some visitor's moorings for those who wish to avail themselves of the delights of StarCity. The landscape is largely uninspiring with a couple of ponds the only relief from the general post-industrial gloom, although the River Rea flows below and unseen, just to the right. The towpath remains solid and provides an easy-going track.

Boaters have no option other than to press on along this stretch as there are no moorings, and other towpath users will probably wish to follow their example. The canal eventually curves slightly to the left at Bridge 108, and the first lock appears shortly after Bridge 107, the foremost of a run of five, the first three of which are close together. In common with all the locks between here and Knowle, these are narrow.

Disused warehouses now dominate, and on approaching Bordesley the canal passes below a number of bridges where there is some evidence of some (mainly residential) regeneration. Some mooring posts allow access to what is called Bordesley Village by Bridge 103. If your sights are set higher, however, there are also some moorings by Bridge 100, allowing access to the nearby Designer Outlet Centre.

Shortly after this, the canal reaches Bordesley Junction, with the Digbeth Branch of the canal to the right, which takes you into Gas Street Basin via a run of fourteen locks. The main line bears left, however, with the Camp Hill flight of six locks following almost immediately, cut in two by the A4540. The towpath reverts to gravel at the second lock, but remains solid. There is a wide sweep to the right between the second and third locks, where a church dominates the skyline up ahead. Facilities including water are available at Camp Hill.

Banana Wharf sits at the top of a long straight, where it is also possible to turn. This passes under Small Heath Bridge, and soon the sweet smell of cut timber pervades the air

> By Bordesley Junction is a large warehouse with an unusually pointed end which originally belonged to the carriers Fellows, Morton & Clayton, as well as another known locally as the Banana Warehouse, as it was used by the fruit importers, Geest.

from a canalside yard. The towpath continues its unbending path past further warehousing and industrial buildings, although, unlike earlier examples, these have the benefit of being in use.

The clock tower of the Marlborough pub looms into view as the towpath passes Sparkbrook. After Bridge 89, there is a rare glimpse of open land on the right, taken up by football pitches, although a high brick wall on the towpath side ensures you don't get fooled into thinking that you've entered countryside. A bend to the left follows and the towpath rises up over a pair of bridges, with the Ackers Centre based at the second.

A familiar straight follows with open land now either side, although the occasional industrial building, including the large Energy From Waste plant on the left, serves to remind you of where you are. A further hump-backed bridge follows, which like its predecessor is ridged, and cyclists are advised to dismount here.

The canal soon curves lazily to the right, passing under Bridge 88 where there is also a turning point. This is but an aberration as a very long straight now follows, taking you through Tyseley, although this is hidden behind a combination of high hedgerows and graffitied fences. Halfway down this straight there is a disused wharf on the right. Some inexpertly laid slabs over some cabling in the towpath can make for a bumpy journey for those on two wheels; that said, the towpath, while becoming increasingly narrow, remains solid.

The surroundings now begin to become noticeably more quiet, and more attractive to local wildlife. Yardley Road Bridge acts as a mini tunnel in the middle of this straight, after which the canal diverts to the right and more open surroundings on the outskirts of Solihull. The Olton district of Solihull sits slightly to the left, hidden from view, although some shops are accessible from Bridge 84.

The canal now enters a deep tree-lined cutting which isolates it from the environs of Solihull. This is a quiet and peaceful stretch for walkers and cyclists, although mooring opportunities remain few and far between for boaters. Most bridges give access to local services in Solihull, after which open countryside appears on both sides on the canal, notably after Bridge 78a.

The canal remains in its cutting and curves gently to the right before climbing back onto the surrounding level and gliding into the exotically named Catherine de Barnes, the first real village on the canal.

PRINCIPAL TOWNS AND VILLAGES ALONG THIS STRETCH

BIRMINGHAM CENTRE:

Although known as the country's second city, when it comes to canals, Birmingham is undoubtedly number one, acting as the focal point for a network of waterways known as the 'Birmingham Canal Navigations', a heritage the city is proud to exploit. Heavy bomb damage during the war led to the destruction of much of the city's industrial heritage and a rash of not always well considered building helped to develop a reputation for stark modernistic architecture, and although much of this no longer exists, the perception had proved hard to shake off.

> The term 'Brum', used to describe Birmingham (whose inhabitants are known as 'Brummies'), is derived from the distinctive local dialect known as 'Brummagem'.

The canal approaches Birmingham from the south-east and passes by or through half a dozen of the city's forty wards before reaching its final destination. Although the districts it passes through may seem to aggregate into one continuous built-up area, they can in fact be separated into distinct areas with their own history, traditions and landmarks, even if these may not always be obvious. These districts, and some of the features that characterise them, are listed below:

ACOCKS GREEN:

Adjacent to the canal, Acock's Green takes its name from the Acock family who established a large house here in the 1500s.

BORDESLEY AND BORDESLEY GREEN:

Although often confused, these are two different areas, with Bordesley at the eastern end of the heart of the city marked by large, often derelict, warehousing.

HALL GREEN:

A distinct district between Birmingham and Solihull, notable for its greyhound stadium.

HAY MILLS:

A largely industrial area straddling the canal to the east of the city, close to the Birmingham Railway Museum

NECHELLS AND NECHELLS GREEN:

An inner city area to the north of the city centre, taking in the northern limit of the canal. The subject of much recent regional and European investment, Nechells suffers from being fragmented by a network of road and rail links and by being sandwiched by industrial estates.

OLTON:
The original site of Solihull, with a number of Edwardian and Victorian houses. A large reservoir and two golf courses add to the area's aura of gentility.

SOUTH YARDLEY:
Sited around a roundabout marking the junction between the A4040 and the A45, South Yardley has a park to the north and a cemetery to the south.

SPARKBROOK:
An area that grew rapidly in the mid-nineteenth century, Sparkbrook is home to a vibrant Asian community whose food and fashion dominates the local shops.

SPARKHILL:
Renowned for its restaurants, particularly along the Ladypool Road, Sparkhill was the location for the city's first Indian restaurant, and the district also has the headquarters of the Wing Yip Chinese supermarket chain.

STETCHFORD:
An unexpectedly green area, due largely to its position in the floodplain of the River Cole, Stetchford is also home to a large retail and leisure complex.

WARD END:
A less than salubrious area, distinguished only by its large park and house.

YARDLEY:
Mentioned in the Domesday Book and busy in Tudor times, parts of Yardley remain a conservation area.

Note: Solihull and Catherine de Barnes are covered in detail in Section B.

HISTORY

Landlocked in the middle of the country, roughly equidistant from the other great port cities of London, Bristol, Manchester/Liverpool and Hull, Birmingham has always seemed a little out on its own and as such has developed a reputation for fierce independence. In recent times, it has also had a reputation as something of a 'concrete jungle', and before that as a heavily industrial area lacking a clear focus.

Like all clichés, these images contain a germ of truth, although Birmingham has worked hard over the last twenty years to reinvent itself as a service-led centre of sport and culture and, while reputations can take a long time to change, the city has been remarkably successful in recasting itself in this new mould. 'Second city' is no longer seen as 'second best'.

It is true to say that Birmingham grew rapidly during the Industrial Revolution and that signs of the largely uncoordinated nature of that growth still help to define the city today. Equally, Birmingham's success during that time led ultimately to it becoming a prime target for Hitler's bombs, necessitating a comprehensive re-build in the 1950s and 1960s, which in turn led to an over-dependence on one style of architecture, one that quickly lost favour.

Bordesley Junction.

It would be a mistake, however, to linger on these two influences, as Birmingham's roots go much deeper. The first references to a settlement here date back to Roman times when there was a fort to protect a crossroads of military routes, although by the time of Domesday, the place was still only a small hamlet with five villagers and four smallholders. Such was its relative unimportance that it was recorded as being worth only 20s.

> Birmingham was first settled by followers of the ingas of Birm or Beorma, and as the place was only a hamlet it gained the suffix 'ham'.

Birmingham's fortunes began to shift 100 years after the invasion in 1166, when Peter de Birmingham, the first man to carry the town's name, bought the right to hold a weekly market in his castle – appropriately in the area that was to become known as the Bullring.

The natural location and existing roads meant that the market prospered, and in 1232 an agreement was reached with William de Birmingham that freed the inhabitants from compulsory haymaking duties, giving them the time to get involved with cloth making, thus initiating Birmingham's long association with industry.

By 1300 the town had grown to become the third largest settlement in Warwickshire, lagging behind Coventry and Warwick, although it had absorbed nearby Aston, which 150 years before had been much more significant. Meanwhile the town continued to trade in cloth, but another commodity had also begun to gain in importance – metal.

The castle remained an important feature of the town, allowing for the incorporation of two new chapels dedicated to the Holy Cross and St John the Baptist, the latter for the inhabitants of Bordesley. A school and Guildhall followed, but by the 1500s the influence of the de Birmingham family began to fade. Edward of that line died in 1538 after four years incarcerated in the Tower of London, and the manor passed to Lord Lisle of nearby Dudley, who was in time to become the Duke of Northumberland and a figure of unchallenged power in the reign of Edward VI.

This was to prove a blessing in disguise for Birmingham. Although on the one hand deprived of a local protector, the town gained relative freedom to develop as it wished. The tradition of independence began to take root.

The town was also blessed with ease of access to iron ore and coal, which led in turn to the development of skills in metalworking. Much of this was delicate work conducted in small workshops rather than organised factories. Small arms became a speciality and as early as 1511 the Clerk of Ordnance was placing orders here for weaponry and the Gun Quarter developed.

From a population of 1,000 in 1500, by the time of the Civil War in the mid-1600s, the town had grown to 7,000. Much of Oliver Cromwell's weaponry was made in Birmingham and the town was firmly Parliamentarian throughout the conflict, despite suffering a raid

> Yardley's church has a doorway surrounded by a pomegranate commemorating the marriage of Prince Arthur, Prince of Wales, in Tudor times, to Catherine of Aragon, later the bride of Arthur's brother, Henry VIII. The doorway also has a collection of Tudor roses.

by Prince Rupert after the king had suffered the indignity of having the royal baggage train looted by the town's inhabitants.

After the conflict, Birmingham became a magnet for immigrants from neighbouring villages. The town had a virtual monopoly on the resources and skills required for metal manufacture, with nails joining the list of articles specialised in. Corn mills were converted for metalwork and, by 1700, the town's population had doubled to 15,000.

This immigration included people coming from areas such as Aston, Olton and Yardley. The last of these had until this time been discrete from Birmingham, having its own mention in the Domesday Book and a Tudor hall called Blakesley Hall, as well as a Tudor church.

> James Brindley's importance to the development of the canal network is recognised by the naming of Brindleyplace in the heart of Birmingham's canal area.

Birmingham was, therefore, perfectly placed to exploit the Industrial Revolution, both in terms of its skill base and geographically in terms of its access to raw materials. Its position in the centre of the country was also turned to its advantage as it formed the natural crossing point of the 'Grand Cross' envisaged by the canal pioneer James Brindley, which linked the four main seaports mentioned above.

> According to his colleague Jesse Collings, Joseph Chamberlain left Birmingham 'parked, paved, assized, marketed, gas and watered and improved'.

Birmingham became Britain's Venice, with the noise and dirt, but without the charm. The canals grew into a spider's web of routes which today are known as the 'Birmingham Canal Navigations'. Raw materials and finished goods passed into and out of the town with ease, and further rapid growth followed.

The railways arrived by 1837, and again, Birmingham became a natural junction for routes heading north, south, east and west. Meanwhile, the town got its act together when the pioneering Liberal Joseph Chamberlain instituted a programme of public works which befitted the granting of city status in 1889, with the population now standing at over half a million. Surrounding districts were absorbed by the city so that it became necessary to grant it its own municipal status, discrete from Warwickshire and Worcestershire, parts of which it had also begun to encroach into.

After the destruction of the Second World War, the city was subject to a fresh wave of immigration, as significant as that from the surrounding hinterland earlier in its history, when it became a favoured location for peoples from the British Commonwealth. This has given Birmingham a rich diversity of culture which has become one the main features of the modern city.

Another feature of the city is its canals, the virtues of which Birmingham was very early to appreciate – it took Manchester two more decades to understand the asset it was sitting on. The second redevelopment of the city after the Second World War, in the 1980s and beyond, was much more considered than the rushed job that followed the immediate aftermath of the conflict, although as was suggested at the beginning of this consideration of the area's history, in some minds Birmingham has still to gain the true credit for this. Despite this, it is difficult to deny that Birmingham, in the early years of the twenty-first century, is an outward looking, dynamic city with much going for it.

THE NATURAL LANDSCAPE

Birmingham itself sits on relatively high ground compared to the surrounding landscape and, as a result, can occasionally be subject to strong winds and even tornados.

The River Rea flows to the west of the canal and then disappears under culverts through the city centre, before reappearing in the Highgate area, while the River Cole to the east is a more defining natural feature with a wide floodplain that prevents build-ing, thereby creating a natural barrier

> In the summer of 2005 the area of Sparkbrook was subject to 135mph winds and a tornado that destroyed many houses. Resulting publicity has led to plans for massive investment in the area, generally seen as economically deprived compared to the rest of Birmingham.

between Stechford and Ward End as well as Hay Mills and Bordesley Green. The river cuts across the canal just east of Bridge 88e. Another river which makes a brief appearance in this section is the Tame to the north, which flows into the Rea at Nechells, while a few small brooks also flow from the north into the canal.

Olton Reservoir is the other main feature involving water and the towpath traveller has to wait until after Bridge 81 until there is any sign of woodland, and even then it is a brief appearance.

ACCESS AND TRANSPORT

ROADS

Birmingham acts as a natural focus for most of the major trunk roads in this area with the A45 joining from Coventry in the east and the A34 from the far south, passing through the city and heading north. The A41 bisects these two and travels down to Solihull, and the A47 passes through Nechells all the way into the centre of Birmingham. The M42 passes to the east of the section and there is a run of the motorway-grade A-road (the A38) heading north out of the city centre.

The city has a ring road (the A4540) and this can be a useful route for passing round the outskirts of the city, although it passes through highly built-up areas and is rarely traffic free. The other main road worth mentioning is the B4128, which passes north of Bordesley Green before meeting the A45 and ring road in the south of Bordesley.

RAIL

Again, Birmingham is a major rail transport hub with two major termini (New Street and Snow Hill). The city's location also means that many cross-country routes pass through it, making Birmingham extremely easy to access by rail. The presence of a number of local stations also means that most of the places in this section are easy to reach by rail.

Routes to London use both the main termini, with Silverlink and Virgin trains using New Street, and Chiltern Railways, Snow Hill. The first two of these go into Euston and tend to be faster while Chiltern go into Marylebone and are more commuter-based. Snow Hill is also used by Central, whose services cover all points of the compass from Birmingham, but in this section head down towards Leamington Spa and spur off towards Stratford. Virgin trains criss-cross the country, with Birmingham acting more as a stop than a terminus.

Stations covered in this section include :

- North-west out of Snow Hill:
  St Pauls
  Jewellery Quarter
- South-east out of Snow Hill:
  Moor Street
  Bordesley
  Small Heath (Sparkhill)
  Tyseley (Hay Mills)
  Acocks Green
  Olton

- North out of New Street:
  Duddeston (Nechells)
  Aston
- East out of New Street:
  Adderley Park (Bordesley Green)
  Stechford
  Lea Hall
  Marston Green
  Birmingham International
- South from Snow Hill via Tyseley:
  Spring Road
  Hall Green

Train operators serving this area are:

- Central Trains (01216 541200)
- Chiltern Railways (01296 332113)
- Virgin Trains (08457 222333)

- Otherwise, National Train Enquiries can be reached on 08457 484950

BUSES

The following list sets out the main bus routes servicing this section, although it is advisable to check before using them as some buses only run on certain days and others may have been withdrawn since publication of this Guide. It is also worth checking for more local services, in particular those within Birmingham itself , where there are a number of circular and school-term-time only services.

- 11A and 11C – *Acocks Green to Stechford*
- 13/15 – *Birmingham to Yardley*
- 17 – *Birmingham to Yardley*
- 30 – *Solihull to Acocks Green via Olton*
- 31 – *Hall Green to City Centre (evenings and Sundays only)*
- 32 – *Acocks Green to Yardley*
- 36 and 36C – *Stechford to Sparkhill*
- 37 – *City centre to Solihull via Sparkbrook, Acocks Green and Olton*
- 41a and 41C – *Solihull to Hall Green*
- 43 – *Acocks Green to City Centre*
- 56 – *Yardley to Birmingham*
- 66 and 66A – *Nechells to City Centre*
- 192/194 – *Acocks Green to Solihull via Olton*

All the above services are operated by Travel West Midlands (0121 254 7272). Traveline (www.traveline.org.uk) on 0870 6082608 can also give details of specific services between 7 a.m. and 10 p.m. The city's main coach station is ten minutes out of the centre at Digbeth.

TAXIS
The following list gives a selection of the taxi operators in this section:

- Arden Cars, Bordesley Green (0121 784 4440)
- B B's Taxis, Central Birmingham (0121 693 3331)
- Blue Arrow Cars, Central Birmingham (0121 622 1000)
- Bromford Cars, Nechells (0121 327 2222)
- City Link Cars, Central Birmingham (0121 666 7000)
- G.T Radio Cars, Bordesley Green (0121 772 1000)
- Five Star Cars, Sparkbrook (0121 685 1111)
- Hall Green Taxis, Hall Green (0121 777 2939)
- Local Cars, Sparkhill (0121 772 8081)
- Manor Cars, Stechford (0121 786 2000)
- Premiere Radio Cars, Acocks Green (0121 783 4444)
- St Pauls Cars, Central Birmingham (0121 233 0303)
- Taxis In Birmingham, Acocks Green (0121 707 4444)

Birmingham is justly proud of its position in the canal system.

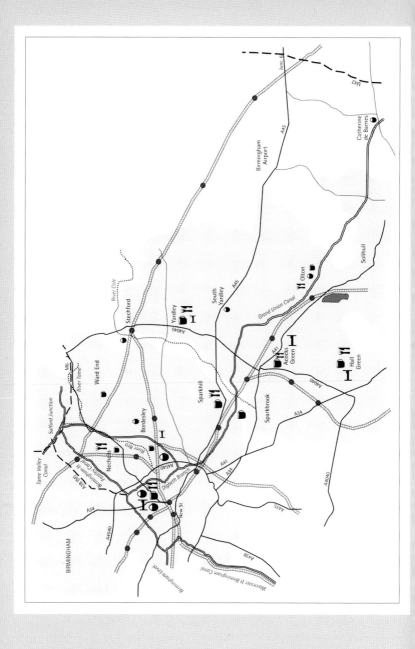

BASICS

INTRODUCTION

Quite reasonably, Birmingham dominates this section, although the canal tends to skirt the eastern edge of the city as it heads south from Salford Junction and, as such, much of what the city has to offer can be hard to access. It is possible, however, to take a right at Bordesley Junction to follow the Digbeth Branch round the western edge of the centre down through the environs of Aston University to the gathering point of Gas Street Basin, from where it is a relatively easy task to access the city itself.

Heartlands Hospital, part of Birmingham Heartlands and Solihull NHS Trust, is based in Bordesley Green (0121 424 2000).

SHOPPING

In recent years Birmingham has put a lot of effort into revitalising its shopping, resulting in a cornucopia of choice scattered around a relatively compact area. For many years, shopping in Birmingham was synonymous with the Bullring Centre which, although cutting edge when it was built in the 1960s, became, by universal acclaim, an ugly eyesore offering a shopping environment out of step with the retail revolution that took place from the 1980s onwards.

In a step typically brave of Birmingham's planners, the entire Centre was demolished and a new one built in its place. Although it shares a name with its predecessor, the new Bullring is an altogether different beast. Whether it, too, will eventually fall victim to changing tastes remains an open question, and the centre's iconic Selfridges building, with its unusual almost Guggenheim-esque exterior made up of 15,000 aluminium discs, is a 'love it or hate it' building.

The Bullring has over 160 stores located near to the Moor Street railway station and, as well as Selfridges, has a Debenhams department store. Practically any large fashion or leisure brand worth its salt has a store here and, as is the modern way, there are also a number of places to stop and snack.

Birmingham is much more than the Bullring, however, and boasts The Mall Pallasades on East Mews, which hosts the less fashionable but still useful end of the High Street such as Woolworths, New Look and Footlocker, and Pavilion Central around New Street station, which has around forty stores including names such as Marks & Spencer, Waterstone's and HMV.

> The Bullring cost over £0.5m a day to build during its construction phase, and contains around a quarter of the total amount of steel in the Empire State Building in New York.

Other Birmingham malls include Martineau Place on Corporation Street, which boasts the largest Gap and Sainsbury's Central in the city, as well as niche suppliers such as extreme sports retailer Free Spirit, and the Great Western Arcade, forty-two shops in a preserved Victorian arcade between Snow Hill and the Bullring, where the accent is on the elegant. Similarly, the City Plaza in Cannon Street has recently been redeveloped into a collection of specialist cutting-edge fashion and accessory shops complete with an art gallery.

The Mailbox on Wharfside Street will be of particular interest to those accessing the city from the towpath, and has fifty fashion and homeware stores, as well as hotels and restaurants. Significantly, it also has Birmingham's Harvey Nichols store as well as other fashion brands such as Boss and Armani.

There is also a House of Fraser and a Beatties in Birmingham, and the pleasant open streets leading through the centre leading up to the town hall mean it is easy to get around. In total, there are over 1,000 shops in the city, with enough of them still owned by independents to allow for some surprises. Examples include Zen (0121 643 3933) on the Water's Edge at Brindleyplace, Nostalgia and Comics (0121 643 0143) on the Queensway and the milliners, If The Cap Fits (0121 224 8456), in The Custard Factory on Gibb Street.

Finally, there's a Farmer's Market every first and third Wednesday in the month at New Street. Also, the Bullring Markets have recently been relaunched, offering a place to buy fresh food ingredients. This has existed for over 800 years and has repositioned itself to attract the general public with not only food but also clothes and other household items sold from market stalls.

> The Birmingham Mint was established by the steam pioneer Matthew Boulton in 1786, who used his new engines to drive coin presses, which up until then had been operated by hand. In this way he made up for the demand for bronze coinage which the Bank of England had proved unable to meet.

Before leaving Birmingham, also worth a mention is the city's Jewellery Quarter, a Conservation Area in recognition of the fact that for 250 years it has been a focus for trading in items of jewellery, gold and diamonds. This is the place to come if you want to shop for an engagement ring, get a watch repaired or simply to browse. It also acts as a tourist destination and is the home to the privately owned Birmingham Mint.

Of course, there are also a number of more local shopping opportunities along this stretch, ranging from small parades serving local communities through to large out-of-centre retail parks. One of the latter is the Stechford Retail Park, which is mainly comprised of discount outlets while another, more upmarket offering is the Trident Retail Park just before Bridge 100 at Bordesley Junction, which has a number of designer outlets.

Before that there is a small local development either side of Bridge 103 at Bordesley, which includes a convenience store and a newsagent. Stechford also has its own local shops on Station Road and Albert Road, while further south, just north of Bridge 84 in Olton, there is another shop and newsagent along with a Chinese takeaway and a launderette.

Distinctive signposts guide you through the BCN.

Other districts each have their own local shops, although these are not always that accessible from the towpath. Worthy of mention, however, is the Beowulf Brewing Co. in Waterloo Road, Yardley (0121 706 4116), which sells firkins of draught beer.

EATING AND DRINKING

As you might expect from such a bustling city, Birmingham has its fair share of pubs, ranging from trendy wine bars to good old-fashioned boozers!

The following lists give a sample of what is available in both Birmingham and the surrounding districts. Inevitably, as throughout this guide, these lists cannot be comprehensive and inclusion on them does not constitute a recommendation. In particular in this section, many will fall into the category of 'town-centre' pubs, the attractions of which may not necessarily be to everyone's taste!

As might be expected, the canal acts as a magnet for many pubs in the city centre, notably at Broad Street, Gas Street Basin and Brindleyplace. These include:

- The Brasshouse (0121 633 3383)
- The Canal Boat Bar (0121 643 2000)
- The Flapper and Firkin (0121 236 2421)
- The Gunmakers Arms (0121 236 1201) – *off the Digbeth Branch*
- The Figure of Eight (0121 633 0917)
- The James Brindley (0121 644 5971)
- The Malt House (0121 633 4171)
- The Pitcher and Piano (0121 633 4171)
- The Pit Stop (0121 644 5981)
- The Tap and Spile (0121 632 5602)
- The Wharf (08701 977 031)

Other pubs around the city centre offering something a bit different include:

- The Anchor, Bradford Street (0121 622 4516) – *classic street corner pub, but child-friendly*
- The Prince of Wales, Cambridge Street (0121 643 9460) – *favoured by members of the City of Birmingham Symphony Orchestra*
- The Square Peg, Corporation Street (0121 236 6530) – *said to have the longest bar in Birmingham*
- Mr Bill's Bier Keller, Exeter Street (0121 354 6652) – *themed pub with oompah band*
- The Windsor, Cannon Street (0121 633 3013) – *town-centre pub squeezed between shops*
- The Mercat, Bradford Street (0121 622 3281) – *early opening hours to suit market traders*
- Scruffy Murphy's, Dale End (0121 236 2035) – *just one of many Irish-themed pubs in Birmingham*
- The Old Joint Stock, Temple Row West (0121 200 1892) – *impressive façade*

Pubs in the various districts approaching Birmingham include the following:

- The Fox and Goose, Ward End (0121 783 2090)
- The Dog and Partridge, Nechells (0121 359 2273)
- Villa Tavern, Nechells (0121 326 7466)
- Samson and Lion, Yardley Green Road, Bordesley Green (0121 766 5943)
- The Tipsy Gent, Cherrywood Road, Bordesley Green (0121 772 1858)
- The Wagon and Horses, Adderley St, Bordesley Green (0121 772 1403)
- The New Inn, Yardley (0121 700 7931)
- The Old Bill and Bull, Yardley (0121 700 7951)
- The Redhill Tavern, Yardley (0121 753 5101)
- The Journey's End, South Yardley (0121 700 7931)
- The Bear Hotel, Sparkhill (0121 702 0921)
- McDwyers, Sparkhill (0121 771 4771)
- Montgomery's, Sparkhill (0121 772 8858)
- The Hereford Arms, Sparkbrook (0121 773 7947)

- The Marlborough, Sparkbrook
  (0121 772 2459)
- The Redhill Tavern, Hay Mills
  (0121 753 5101)
- The Gospel Oak, Acocks Green
  (0121 777 0709)
- The Lady Westminster, Acocks
  Green (0121 708 0104)
- The Spread Eagle, Acocks Green
  (0121 708 0194)
- The Lincoln Poacher, Olton
  (0121 706 5429)
- The Baldwin Arms, Hall Green
  (0121 744 3356)
- The Bulls Head, Hall Green
  (0121 702 0931)
- The Horseshoe, Hall Green
  (0121 777 2340)
- The Three Magpies, Hall Green
  (0121 777 8444)

Marlborough Arms, Sparkbrook.

- The York, Hall Green (0121 702 0961)

When it comes to eating, the question is where to start? Given the focus of this book, the answer probably lies with Brindleyplace, a business, retail and leisure resource grouped around Gas Street Basin. Towpath travellers can access all they need from this one place, but it also acts as a convenient jumping off point into the city centre.

At a basic level, there is a Sainsbury's Local and a Spar here, as well as sandwich stores, a Boots, an art gallery and the aforementioned Zen, selling alternative lifestyle products. Critically, there are also thirty restaurants, including:

- Bank (0121 633 4466) – *French/
  British*
- Café Ikon (0121 248 3226)
  – *Spanish*
- Delizzi (0121 643 5553)
  – *Mediterranean*
- Pizza Express (0121 643 2500)
  – *Italian*
- Shogun Teppan-Yaki (0121 643
  1856) – *Japanese/Sushi*
- Thai Edge (0121 643 3993) – *Thai*

Also based around the Basin are:

- Away2Eat (0845 644 5244)
  – *restaurant boat*
- Canalside Cottage (0121 248 7979)
  – *café*
- Floating Coffee Company, nb
  George (0121 633 0050) – *coffee*

As already mentioned, the various malls also offer a number of places to snack, while the Mailbox is more restaurant-based and offers a more substantial dining experience with examples including:

- Santa Fe (0121 632 1250) – *Mexican*
- Paris (0121 632 1488) – *run by a
  Michelin-starred chef*
- Don Salvo (0121 643 4000) – *Italian*
- Paxton and Whitfield
  (0121 632 1440) – *meals using
  cheeses sold in this store*

The first Indian restaurant in Birmingham was opened by Abdul Aziz in Steelhouse Lane, Sparkhill, as a café shop selling curry and rice. Success led to the café becoming a restaurant known as The Darjeeling.

A feature of Birmingham's restaurants is their diversity, and in 2004 the city won the EthniCity award in recognition of this fact. On the basis that half the fun is in the chase, the visitor is probably best advised to seek out their own venue according to individual preference. If you prefer to be guided, however, the following represents a selection of what is on offer:

- Athens, Paradise Circus (0121 6435523) – *Greek*
- Al Frash Balti, Ladypool Road (0121 753 3120) – *Balti*
- Chung Ling, Thorpe Street (0121 666 6622) - *Chinese*
- Dragon, Broadway Plaza (0121 4563166) – *Chinese BBQ*
- Henry's Cantonese, St Paul's Square (0121 200 1136) – *Chinese*

- Ipanema, Broad Street (0121 643 5577) – *Latin American*
- Lasan, James Street (0121 212 3664) – *Indian*
- Punjab Paradise, Ladypool Road (0121 4494110) – *Balti*
- Shogun Sushi and Noodle Bar, Wharfside Street (0121 632 1253) – *Japanese*
- Xaymaca Experience, Bristol Street (0121 6223332) – *Jamaican*

If you want something slightly less exotic, you may wish to explore one of the following:

- City Café, Brunswick Square (0121 643 1003) – *a là carte dining*
- Green Room, Hurst Street (0121 605 4343) – *vegetarian*
- Henry J Beans, Broad Street (0121 643 7222) – *American*

- Old Joint Stock, Temple Row West (0121 200 1892) – *superior pub food*
- Talk Bar, Cannon Street (0800 0790909) – *English*
- Zinc Bar and Grill, Regency Wharf (0121 200 0620)

On the way out of Birmingham the choice tends to narrow to the Asian cuisines, although not exclusively. The following is a sample of possible stopping-off places:

- Mint Cuisine, Yardley (0121 789 8908) – *Indian*
- Thai Wai, Yardley (0121 722 3338) – *Thai*
- Jyoti, Sparkhill (0121 766 7199) – *vegetarian Indian*
- The President, Sparkhill (0121 772 7786) – *Indian*
- Somali Restaurant, Sparkhill (0121 687 0070) – *Somali*
- Pasta di Piazza, Acocks Green

  (0121 707 0221) – *Italian*
- Hot Food Paradise, Olton (0121 707 1888) – *Chinese takeaway*
- Da Marco, Hall Green (0121 778 3299) – *Italian*
- Liaison Restaurant, Hall Green (0121 733 7336) – *French*
- Royal Balti Hut, Hall Green (0121 236 8664) – *Indian*
- Shaftmoor, Hall Green (0121 777 5415) – *Chinese takeaway*

In addition, the Star City Leisure Complex at Nechells has a number of themed diners, including:

- Nandos (0121 327 8551)
- Old Orleans (0121 327 8275)

- Ma Potters Char Grill (0121 328 9696)
- La Tasca (0121 327 8223)

SLEEPING

HOTELS

Unsurprisingly, as a major conference and sporting location, Birmingham has a good selection of hotels, ranging from the large four- and five-star chains through to more modest two- and three-star hotels, some of which are independently owned.

Those at the more expensive end of the spectrum in the city centre include:

- The Burlington Hotel, New Street (0121 643 9191)
- Copthorne Hotel, Paradise Place, Jewellery Quarter (0121 200 2727)
- Crowne Plaza, Broad Street (0121 631 2000)
- Holiday Inn, Smallbrook Queensway (0870 400 9008)
- Hotel du Vin, Church Street, Jewellery Quarter (0121 236 0559)

- *– located in the old Birmingham Eye Hospital*
- Hyatt Regency, Bridge Street (0121 643 1234)
- Malmaison Hotel, Wharfside Street (0121 246 5000)
- Novotel, Broad Street (0121 643 2000)
- Thistle, St Chads, Queensway (0870 333 9126)

More budget-level Birmingham hotels include:

- Briar Rose, Bennetts Hill (0121 634 8100)
- Britannia Hotel, New Street (0121 631 3331)
- Campanile Hotel, Chester Street (0121 359 3330) – *near Aston Locks*
- City Inn, Broad Street (0121 643 1003) – *on Brindleyplace*
- Days Inn, Wharfside Street (0121 643 9344)

- Formule 1, Bordesley Park (0121 773 9583)
- Hotel Ibis, Irving Street (0121 622 4925)
- Travel Inn, Bridge Street (0121 633 4820)
- Travelodge, Broad Street (0870 191 1564)
- The Wellington Hotel, Bristol Street (0121 622 2592)

As might be expected, hotels away from the centre of Birmingham tend to be less expensive, with a tendency for them to group around Acocks Green and Halls Green. The following is a selection of those available:

- Ibis, Bordesley (0121 506 2600)
- Travelodge, Yardley (0870 0850950)
- Avalon Hotel, Acocks Green (0121 708 2177)
- Boss House Hotel, Acocks Green (0121 707 8778)
- Bridge House Hotel, Acocks Green (0121 706 5900)
- The Coach House Hotel, Acocks Green (0121 706 1088)
- Elmdon Guest House, Acocks Green (0121 706 9583)

- Greenway House Hotel, Acocks Green (0121 706 1361)
- Greswolde Park Hotel, Acocks Green (0121 706 4068)
- Westley Hotel, Acocks Green (0121 706 4312)
- Express by Holiday Inn, Hall Green (0121 744 4414)
- The Lodge, Hall Green Stadium, Hall Green (0121 777 3480)
- Robin Hood Lodge Hotel, Hall Green (0121 778 5307)

BED AND BREAKFAST/GUEST HOUSES

Bed and breakfasts and guest houses are not thick on the ground in this part of Birmingham, with most congregating in the leafier areas of the city. The airport exercises some degree of pull, however, as does the opening up of the landscape further south. The following list offers a selection of what is available:

- Elston B&B, Ward End (0121 327 3338)
- Bluebell Guest House, Yardley (0121 707 3232)
- Gables Nest, South Yardley (0121 708 2712)
- Olton Cottage Guest House, Yardley (0121 783 9249)
- Yardley Guest House, Yardley (0121 783 6634)
- Central Guest House, South Yardley (0121 706 7757)

- Atholl Lodge, Acocks Green (0121 707 4417)
- Holly House Hotel, Acocks Green (0121 706 1211)
- Penshurst, Acocks Green (0121 707 8798)
- Williamson B&B, Acocks Green (0121 708 0585)
- Corner House B&B, Halls Green (0121 744 4721)

CAMPING

Unsurprisingly, perhaps, this is not a good stretch for camping. The nearest site is probably the one run by the Camping and Caravanning Club at Clents Hills in Halesowen (01562 710015). It is possible to access supplies in central Birmingham:

- Bailey, The Pallasades, Birmingham (0121 643 4787)
- Blacks, Bull Street, Birmingham (0121 233 1678)

- Millets, New Street, Birmingham (0121 643 0885)
- Millets, Union Street, Birmingham (0121 643 1496)

Bordesley Junction.

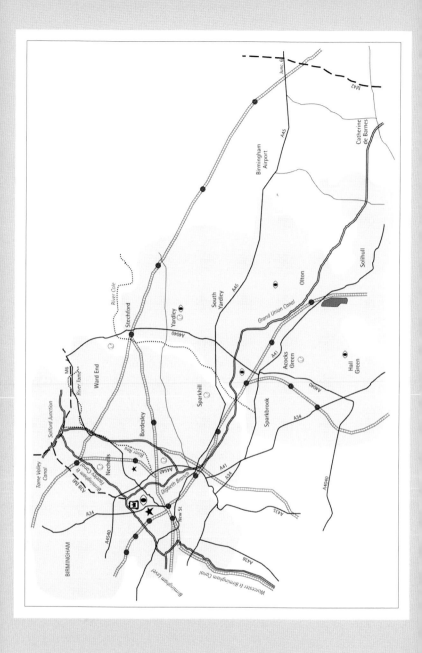

Key

 Canal

 River

Railway

— — — Motorway

A Road

B Road

Built up area

Stations

Open water

Site/Sight

Leisure

Entertainment

Culture

SEEING AND DOING

INTRODUCTION

It may come as a surprise to some, but it is perfectly possible to spend a long weekend in Birmingham and still run out of time to cover all that the city has to offer. The canals, not just the Grand Union, have become a major feature, and the city has worked hard to make itself a destination of choice for visitors.

While there are sights to see outside the centre, most of the attractions sit within comfortable walking distance of each other and towpath travellers will find the city's relative compactness convenient, and will also appreciate the fact that it is possible to visit many of the attractions for free.

The main Tourist Information Centre is based at the Rotunda in New Street (0870 428 1859).

SIGHTS

A walk taking in many of Birmingham's historic buildings is featured in the 'Sampling' section, and offers a good way to orientate oneself when first visiting the city.

Birmingham's Cathedral of St Philip is unmissable, sitting proud in the heart of the city in the middle of its own square off Colmore Row. The building is Grade I listed and was designed by Thomas Archer in the English Baroque style, being built between 1709 and 1715. It was granted Cathedral status in 1905 when the Diocese of Birmingham was formed. Inside, look out for four Pre-Raphaelite stained-glass windows by Sir Edward Burne-Jones.

Mention has already been made of Brindleyplace near Centenary Square, which has rapidly become one of the city's main focal points. As well as the International Convention Centre and National Indoor Arena, this

Second City Canal Cruises (0121 236 9811) offer public guided tours from their boats *Europe* and *Dragonfly*, and also have a canal souvenir shop in Gas Street Basin. A greater accent on Birmingham's past is offered by Sherborne Wharf Heritage Narrowboats (0121 455 6163), which operates three boats through the industrial heart of the city.

is also the location of the National Sealife Centre (0121 643 6777) with its tubular underwater walk-through tunnel complete with the inevitable sharks.

The city also has its own, more modest, version of London's Millennium Eye, the Wheel of Birmingham in Centenary Square (0845 055 6080) which has forty-two capsules seating between six and eight people. Also of interest to families will be the Thinktank Museum of Science and Discovery in Curzon Street (0121 202 2222), home to the city's IMAX cinema and a Planetarium as well as ten galleries' worth of hands-on exhibits.

As well as being a centre for shopping and eating, The Mailbox (0121 632 1000) off Commercial Street is also home to the BBC in the Midlands, and it is possible to watch programmes being made here through a glass window which peers into the studios.

Birmingham Museum and Art Gallery (0121 303 2834) on Chamberlain Square also has a Pre-Raphaelite collection as well as collections of silver, ceramics and sculpture, and also the Waterhall Gallery which focuses on modern art from the city's collection.

The West Midlands Police Museum (0121 626 7181) in Sparkhill Police Station holds occasional open days during which it exhibits its collection and allows visitors to see the cells.

The Jewellery Quarter to the north-west of the centre is worth mentioning in its own right. A century ago, over 30,000 Brummies were involved in the jewellery trade. Today, the quarter has a number of historic buildings, including factories and workships, a former electro-plating works, period houses and the Birmingham Assay Office. Pavement trails are set out to allow visitors to explore.

Birmingham's dominance in pens owes a lot to Jospeh Gillott, who perfected a technique for manufacturing steel nibs by machine. His contribution was more than commercial as mass production helped to spread literacy to the working classes.

Birmingham's Assay Office uses an anchor as its symbol. Legend suggests that the choice was made on the toss of a coin in a pub called the Crown and Anchor, with the symbol of the crown won by Sheffield.

The Museum of the Jewellery Quarter (0121 554 3598) offers a guided tour of a jewellery factory and gives the background to the city's role in the trade, from the Middle Ages to the present day. There is usually a live demonstration of jewellery making.

The Jewellery Quarter is also home to St Paul's Square, a Georgian delight and the location of St Paul's church, built in 1779, which was the place of worship for both James Watt and his contemporary Matthew Boulton – whose pew was number 23! Also located in the Quarter is the Pen Room (0121 236 9834), a museum of writing and the pen trade, another of the specialist areas Birmingham dominated for more than a century.

An often missed destination in Birmingham is the Back to Backs (0121 666 7671), run by the National Trust and located in Inge and Hurst Streets. This is a collection of the restored homes of four families, each relating to a different time period: 1840s, 1870s, 1930s and 1970s. At one time there were 40,000 such houses in Birmingham and one is preserved as a 'time capsule' for visitors to appreciate living conditions at that time. There is also a 1930s sweet shop which sells sweets from the period.

Other museums include Sarehole Mill (0121 777 6612) in Hall Green, an example of more than fifty such water mills that used to exist in Birmingham and one of many that was converted from grinding corn to industrial use. Sarehole's significance is that it was rented by the father of the industrial pioneer Matthew Boulton, and was later used by Matthew for making buttons and metal rolling.

Also worth a visit is Blakesley Hall in Yardley (0121 464 2193), one of the last surviving timer-framed farmhouses in Birmingham and one time home to wealthy yeoman farmer Richard Smalbroke. Both Blakesley and Sarehole are run by the local council and are free to enter. Another curiosity outside the centre, although one requiring more imagination to appreciate, is the Three

> Sarehole is mentioned in J.R.R. Tolkien's *The Lord of the Rings* and the local village is thought to be the inspiration for Hobbiton and the Shire, the author having grown up around here.

> Ghost and other walks are run by Birmingham Walks 0121 458 5909, and details are available from Tourist Information.

Magpies, a pub in Hall Green. This has a sister pub in the area called the Baldwin, with both designed by Edwin Reynolds. A profile of the front elevation of the two pubs placed side by side with the Three Magpies on the left would reveal the profile of the Cunard liner *The Queen Mary*.

Birmingham Railway Museum (0121 708 4962), just off Bridge 88, is housed in an old Great Western Railway shed and houses the Tyseley Collection of railway artefacts, as well as a number of old locomotives, including the *Stratford-on-Avon*.

Green space is not as plentiful in Birmingham as it is in comparable cities, although slightly out of town in Olton there is the Hobs Moat Ancient Monument, a twelfth-century fortified manor house with a rectangular earthwork surrounding it. The city puts its network of towpaths forward as quiet spaces for those wanting to get away from it all.

Salford Junction looking up.

CULTURE AND ENTERTAINMENT

The Starcity Leisure Complex (0871 230 0013) near the start of the canal has a multiplex cinema, casino and Megabowl, as well as fast-food restaurants and a mini snow slope, climbing wall and Chamber of Horrors. Similarly, the less impressive Arcadian Centre on Hurst Street (0121 622 5348) has restaurants and a dedicated Chinese shopping street as well as a comedy club.

> Known as The Blues, Birmingham City was formed in 1875 by a group of cricketers from Holy Church in Bordesley Green, although they were originally known as the Small Heath Alliance. In 1931 they played in an all-Birmingham FA Cup Final, losing out to West Bromwich Albion.

Birmingham is proud to boast that it stages more national and international sporting championships than any other UK city, and has a central telephone number covering sporting events in the city: 0121 202 5099.

There are three professional football clubs in the immediate vicinity: Aston Villa, Birmingham City and West Bromwich Albion, all of which at the time of writing were in the Premiership, although the position of more than one was precarious! However, only Birmingham City lies within the area covered by this section (0121 772 0101).

The city also has a professional Rugby Union side, Moseley RFC (0121 414 2718), as well as professional basketball with the Birmingham Bullets (0870 766 1647), boxing, hockey, skateboarding and greyhound racing. The latter takes place at the Hall Green Stadium (0121 777 1181).

If you want to get more active yourself, it may be a disappointment to discover that most of the leisure centres lie outside the centre and most of these have a local community focus, including:

- Heartlands High Community Leisure Centre, Nechells (0121 359 7315)
- Foxhollies Leisure Centre, Acocks Green (0121 464 4112)
- Nechells Community Sports Centre (0121 464 4373)
- Ninestiles Community Leisure Centre, Acocks Green (0121 464 4112)
- Saltley Community Leisure Centre, Bordesley Green (0121 464 8556)
- Sparkhill Pool and Fitness Centre (0121 464 1873)
- Stechford Cascades (0121 464 5596) – *pool with flumes*
- Yardley School and Fitness Centre (0121 464 7785)

Slightly out of town and right on the towpath by Bridge 88E, is the Ackers Ski and Snowboard Centre (0121 772 5111), with a 100m floodlit bristle matting slope and two nursery slopes, all set within a 70-acre semi-rural site. The site also has a climbing wall and access to canoeing and its own narrowboat, the Sparkbrook. In a similar vein, there is the Solihull Ice Rink in Hobs Moat Road (0121 742 5561), which has an ice pad, café and skate shop.

The city has four cinemas in addition to the multiplex at Starcity:

> The Electric is the oldest working cinema in the country and, as well as showing more art house films, is a centre for film-making.

- The Electric Cinema, Station Street (0121 643 7879)
- IMAX, Curzon St (0121 202 2222)
- Odeon, New Street (0871 224 4007)
- UGC, Broad St (0870 907 0710)

Birmingham has a number of theatres, ranging from the commercial to the art house, attracting international acts, West End musicals and more experimental drama. Venues include:

- The Alexandra Theatre, Station Street (0121 632 6841) – *a leading touring theatre*
- Birmingham Hippodrome, Hurst Street (0870 730 1234) – *recently refurbished and home to the Birmingham Royal Ballet as well as DanceXchange hosting ballet, musicals, opera and, yes, even panto*
- Birmingham Repertory Theatre, Centenary Square (0121 236 4455) *– producing theatre with a varied programme ranging from classic to contemporary drama to dance hosted in its main theatre and studio*
- Birmingham Stage Company, Old Rep Theatre, Station Street (0121 643 9050) – *professional company*
- The Crescent Theatre, Brindleyplace (0121 643 5858) – *drama*

Art lovers will not be disappointed with galleries scattered around the city. As well as the gallery within Birmingham Museum and those mentioned in the 'Basics' section, there is:

- The Ikon Gallery, Brindleyplace (0121 248 0708) – *words like 'contemporary' and 'progressive' are used to describe this free gallery by the canal*
- The New Gallery, St Paul's Square (0121 223 0800) – *art for sale from modern artists*
- Number Nine, Brindleyplace (0121 643 9099) – *paintings, glass, ceramics and sculpture with an accent on Midlands-based artists*
- Royal Birmingham Society of Artists, St Paul's (0121 236 4353) – *educational and saleroom featuring local talent*

Music lovers will appreciate the City of Birmingham Symphony Orchestra, perhaps most famous for its time under the stewardship of Sir Simon Rattle, which plays at the Symphony Hall (0121 780 3333).

Nightlife in Birmingham is varied, as you might expect, with a number of clubs and bars open until the small hours. These include:

> Perhaps Birmingham's most unusual sculpture is the Sleeping Iron Giant in Olton by Ondre Nowakoski, a giant head on its side, the nose of which is regularly painted blue by fans of nearby Birmingham City FC, who are known as 'blue noses'.

- Air, Bordesley (0121 766 8400) – *home to Godskitchen*
- The Jam House, St Paul's Square (0121 200 3030) – *a popular venue near the Jewellery Quarter supported by the music legend and TV presenter Jools Holland*
- The Custard Factory, Gibb Street (0121 693 6333) – *varied programme*
- Dance Factory, Digbeth (0121 236 8339)
- Flares, Broad Street (0121 632 5501)
- The Que Club, Corporation Street (0121 212 0550)
- The Sanctuary, Digbeth (0121 246 1010)
- The Works, Broad Street (0121 633 1520) – *R'n'B through to garage*
- Zinc, Gas St Basin (0121 200 0620)

The Glee in Hurst Street (0870 241 5093) and Jongleurs in Broad Street (0870 787 0707) are two Comedy Clubs which run from Thursday to Saturday.

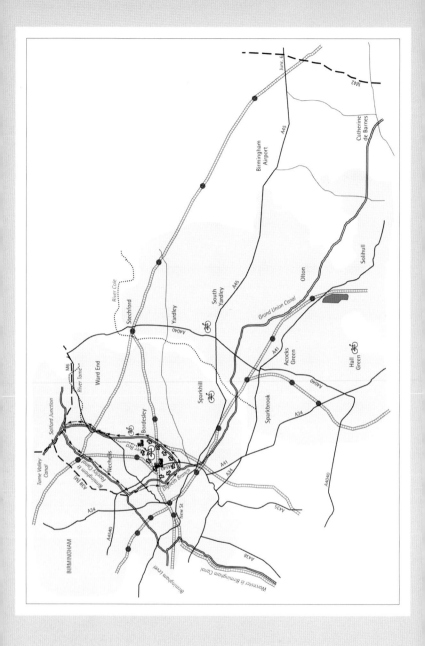

Key

══════	Canal
··············	River
▥▥▥▥▥	Railway
▬ ▬ ▬	Motorway
──────	A Road
──────	B Road

🅿 Built up area

🔴 Stations

🔵 Open water

🚲➜ Cycling route/outlet

🚶⇨ Walking route/outlet

🐟 Fishing spot/outlet

⛳ Golf course/outlet

♘ Riding outlet

SAMPLING

INTRODUCTION

The heavily built-up nature of this section makes it difficult to sample, with the towpath often offering the best through routes. The River Cole flood plain relieves the unremitting concrete and bricks a little but, unfortunately, is not that easy to access.

The section is covered by OS Explorer Map 220, Birmingham.

WALKING

The main formal path along this stretch is the Solihull Way, and the section of this that leads broadly southwards from the River Cole along the Kingfisher Brook and Hatchford Brook as far as the A45 is known as the Kingfisher Way. After the A45 this becomes the Solihull Way again, which bears east on reaching the canal before heading south again at Bridge 78A. Part of the Kingfisher Way also skirts Sheldon Country Park, just west of the airport.

Walk A takes in some of the historic buildings and main sights in Birmingham and acts as a good way to get the feel of the city before going out to explore it more fully. Many of the places covered in the walk are described in more detail in the 'Seeing and Doing' section.

> 122 and 124 Colmore Row on Walk A are architecturally significant because they act as a bridge between the Arts and Crafts Movement and modern styles.

Salford Junction.

SECTION A WALK
Around the City from Gas Street Basin

Description:	*A city stroll taking in parts of the canal*
Distance:	*2 miles*
Duration:	*1 hour*
Starting point:	*Grid Reference 063866, OS Explorer 220, Birmingham*
Nearest refreshment:	*Any of the pubs, bars and cafés in Brindleyplace*

Start by the sign welcoming you to the heart of the canal network by the towpath to the west of Broad Street, near to Edwards restaurant. Follow the towpath and cross over the canal at the bridge into Brindleyplace Square. Head to the left and Oozells Street where you will find the Ikon Gallery. Retrace your steps and head for the National Sea Life Centre, heading back towards the canal.

Cross over the bridge that takes you to the National Indoor Arena and turn right, following the towpath up the Birmingham and Fazeley Canal, which is signposted on the roundabout in the middle of the canal. Follow this down the flight of locks until you reach Snow Hill Bridge. Cross over this and bear right down Livery Street, turning right at Colmore Row. Follow this for a short while and St Philip's Cathedral will be in front of you. Look out also for 122 and 124 Colmore Row. Cross over the square and head down Cherry Union Street, turning right at Corporation Street and left down New Street, taking you to the Rotunda.

Head up the High Street and Dale End, returning to Corporation Street, where you will be met by the Victoria Law Courts. Pass back down Corporation Street all the way back to New Street and turn right. Pass Bennetts, a one-time bank with Corinthian-style pillars, until you are faced by the Renaissance-style Council House. The Museum and Art Gallery is to the left. Keep going straight ahead with the museum behind you. This brings you past the Hall of Memory, an octagonal memorial made of Portland Stone, and then the Repertory Theatre, before returning to the canal.

The Rotunda is a reminder of the 1960s architecture that once dominated Birmingham's centre and is scheduled to stay.

Walking equipment outlets along this section include:
- Blacks, Bull Street (0121 233 1678)
- Millets, New Street (0121 643 0885)
- Millets, Union Street (0121 643 1496)
- Bailey, The Pallasades (0121 643 4787)

CYCLING

Some routes are available for cyclists along this section, although this is not a terribly cycle-friendly area. Plans are afoot to develop routes along the Kingfisher Way, which is nominally part of the Sustrans Route 53 from Birmingham to Rugby, but this is still a work in progress.

The best way to sample this section on two wheels is to stick to the towpaths, with a short (5-mile) circular route possible from Bordesley Junction heading north to Salford Junction, taking a left turn and heading back down the Birmingham and Fazeley Canal as far as Aston Junction. Turn left here and follow the Digbeth Branch via Typhoo Basin back to your starting point.

Cycle outlets along this section include:

- 20 24 26, The Custard Factory, Gibb Street (0121 246 2426)
- A-Z Bikes, Sparkhill (0121 777 1223)
- Birmingham City Cycles, Bristol Street (0121 666 6045)
- Hawk Factory Cycle Stores, Yardley (0121 742 3332)
- Ladypool Cycle Co, Ladypool Road (0121 449 9988)
- On Your Bike, Bradford Street (0121 666 6933)
- Scott Cycles, Hall Green (0121 777 2532)

Steps at the Camp Hill Lock.

RIDING

Perhaps unsurprisingly, this is not an area rich in riding opportunities. Schools, stables and suppliers tend to exist outside the area covered in this section, and riders are recommended to refer to Section B (Sampling).

FISHING

The closest anglers may get to fishing in this section is to go to the Go Fishing show at the NEC in March. There is some fishing around Salford Junction under the auspices of the Newmount AC (0121 711 1667), but the waters south of here are not that inviting. Things perk up a little after Bordesley Junction, but the casual angler is probably best advised to head south of Catherine de Barnes (see Section B).

Outlets selling fishing supplies along this stretch include:
- Acocks Green Angling Centre (0121 706 4477)
- Fisherman's Knockout, Hall Green (0121 777 0307)
- Fox Hollies Exchange (0121 764 6263)
- Rogers Gun and Game Fishing Tackle (0121 706 6387)
- William Powell Fishing Tackle, Carrs Lane (0121 643 8362)
- West Midlands Angling Centre, Ward End (0121 327 4193)

OTHER

There are two opportunities for golf in this section, both full-sized courses:
- Olton Golf Club (0121 704 1936) – *18 holes, 6,229 yards*
- Robin Hood Golf Club (0121 706 0159) – *18 holes, 6,635 yards on flat parkland*

SECTION B

CATHERINE DE BARNES TO HATTON GREEN

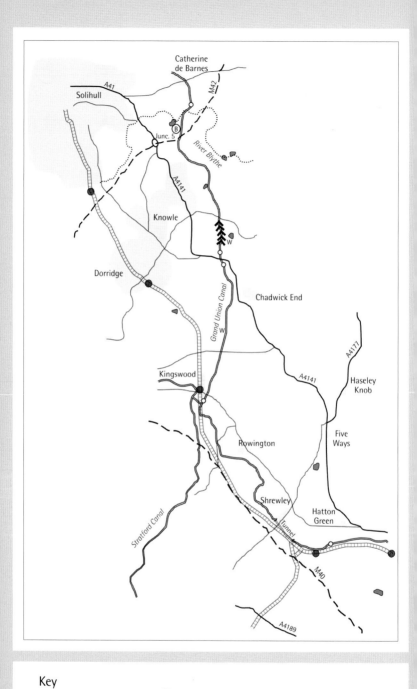

Key

═══	Canal	● Built up area		○	Turning point
··········	River	● Stations		▲	Lock
▦▦▦	Railway	● Open water		Ⓑ	Boatyard
─ ─ ─	Motorway			W	Waterpoint
━━━	A Road				
───	B Road				

Solihull
Catherine de Barnes
A41
M42
Junc. 5
River Blythe
A4141
Knowle
Dorridge
Chadwick End
Grand Union Canal
A4177
Kingswood
A4141
Haseley Knob
Rowington
Five Ways
Stratford Canal
Shrewley
Hatton Green
Tunnel
M40
A4189

SHAPERS

THE CANAL ON THIS STRETCH

KEY FACTS:

LENGTH: 11.75 miles

BOATYARDS: 2
> Copt Heath Wharf
> Stephen Goldsborough Boat, Knowle Hall Wharf

WATER POINTS: 3
> Above Knowle Locks
> Below Knowle Locks
> Rising Bridge (No.66)

TURNING POINTS: 5
> After Henwood Bridge (No.77)
> After Kixley Bridge (No.72)
> Kings Arms Bridge (No.70)
> Kingswood Junction
> St John's Bridge (No.55)

LOCKS: 5
> Knowle Locks (5) (41ft 10in)

The canal quickly exits Birmingham and after Catherine de Barnes skirts first Solihull and then Knowle, although the only locks on this section are named after this small village/town. Long straight sections precede the junction with the Stratford-on-Avon Canal at Kingswood, shortly after which there is the short Shrewley Tunnel and the run in to the dramatic Hatton Flight.

After the urban landscape of Section A, Catherine de Barnes can be an inviting place to stop and mooring rings are conveniently provided for boaters to do so, while the nearby pub and shop are also tempting. Immediately after the village, the towpath loses much of its previous good definition and becomes more of a traditional narrow earth strip and, after a short straight, the canal executes a clear turn to the right before starting a determined path southwards.

A slight kink in the course of the canal precedes Bridge 77, where there is also a turning point. Noise from the nearby Birmingham Airport now becomes more noticeable, but not enough to be intrusive. The water sits on an embankment along the long straight that follows, much of which is occupied by long-term moorings.

The towpath regains some of its previous firmness, with some visitors' moorings just before Copt Heath Wharf, and there is a short

> Day-boat hire, including the vessel *Imp*, is available from Copt Heath Wharf (0121 704 4464).

run of concrete as the canal passes beneath the M42, with the towpath picking up on this trend the other side by becoming noticeably more solid.

The canal now passes through some pleasant countryside with gentle curves punctuating longer straights, whilst continuing a steady drift south. A distinct bend to the right takes place after Bridge 74, however, with another after the following bridge.

The towpath can become quite bumpy in patches in the run up to the five-lock Knowle Flight, which is itself preceded by Knowle Hall Wharf. This is quite a sight, with broad pounds and the beginning of the wide locks (capable of taking two boats side by side) that mark the canal from this point in, although it is still possible to make out where the old narrow locks used to be. Water is available at the top and bottom of this flight, and there is a turning point just after the bottom lock.

A run of long-term moorings follows the locks, after which the elegant Heron's Nest pub appears on the opposite side of the towpath, followed by a winding hole. For those unwilling to cross over the canal for a drink, the Black Boy is also available by Bridge 69. In between the two, the boats of the Black Buoy Cruising Club line both sides of the towpath, with some ringed visitors' moorings at the end.

The landscape to the right opens up here and the towpath briefly becomes an asphalt drive leading up to the pretty half-timbered Haycock Farm. This improvement is only temporary as the path loses much of its previously good definition shortly after. The towpath crosses over at Bridge 67, after which the canal curves slightly to the left.

This is another pleasant rural stretch of canal offering peace and solitude, although there are few places to stop and visit until you reach Lapworth. There is a water point by Bridge 66, and a run of long-term moorings on the opposite bank, with the canal itself stretching out ahead for some distance here, offering tunnel vision down tree-lined banks.

> Kingswood Junction opened in 1803 when a short arm was built from Lapworth on the Stratford Canal to link up with what we know today as the Grand Union. After a feud between the two canal companies, this was filled in and was only reopened in 1995.

The Navigation pub sits by Bridge 65, after which it is possible for boaters to moor up all the way up to and beyond Kingswood Junction, where it is possible to turn. A long, lazy sweep to the left now follows, with concrete-lined banks giving a clean, crisp look to the sides. Sinking into deep contemplation at this point is not advised, however, as the railway runs right next to you on the right and an unexpected train can break your reverie with a start! Around Kingswood, keep an eye out for small orange plaques giving interesting facts about the canal.

Mooring is clustered around the canalside Tom O'The Wood pub at Rowington (Bridge 62), after which the canal wriggles a bit south of Rowington before briefly heading out east, resuming a south-east direction after Bridge 61. Once again, the towpath can get a little bumpy here, but it is a temporary aberration. Passage is now along a tree-lined cutting, but the dappled light comes at a cost for towpath users who will find that this stretch can be quite muddy at all times of the year.

The railway, briefly lost, now comes alongside once again, as does the M40, as all three transport routes exploit the same topography. The canal raises itself up on an embankment and after Bridge 61 takes on an almost aqueduct-like appearance, narrowing considerably as it passes a Christmas-tree nursery.

Bridges 60 and 59 mark a short run up to the modest (433 yards) Shrewley Tunnel where the towpath rises up and passes through its own mini-portal.

SECTION B

> Shrewley Tunnel is notorious for its leaks, so boaters are advised to wear waterproof clothing when passing through. The rock formation at the western end of the tunnel has led to it being designated a site of special scientific interest.

Sadly, this covers only the beginning of the tunnel and is quite steep, with steps near the top. On emerging onto a road, the towpath crosses over and down a track, following the line of the tunnel before picking up the canal once again.

Another wooded cutting appears, although this one is shallower than its processor. Bridge 58 bisects a straight which ends with a curve to the left, after which the boats of the Mid Warwickshire Yacht Club line the bank. Hatton railway station by Bridge 56 then marks the end of this section.

PRINCIPAL TOWNS AND VILLAGES ALONG THIS STRETCH

CATHERINE DE BARNES:
A small scattered village apart from nearby Solihull, with a pub and not one, but two organic farm shops.

CHADWICK END:

> The area near Chadwick End used to be known as Bedlam or Bedlam's End.

Although its name originally meant 'farm near a village', these days Chadwick End is a roadside village on the A4141. It is significant for marking the boundary between Solihull and Warwickshire.

DORRIDGE:
A pleasant suburban outpost of Solihull, clustered around its station, with some large open spaces and plenty of mature trees.

FIVE WAYS:
A tiny hamlet whose main and perhaps only claim to fame is sitting on the junction of the five routes featured in its name.

HASELEY KNOB:
A pleasant if unremarkable small village just off the A4147, approached from one direction via a long tree-lined boulevard.

HATTON GREEN:
A small, linear hamlet comprising desirable housing.

KINGSWOOD:
A small, canalside settlement tucked into the crook of the meeting of the Grand Union with the Stratford Canal and home to Lapworth station.

KNOWLE:
A vibrant market town which easily retains its own identity despite being on the edge of the much larger Solihull with a liberal sprinkling of older buildings and architectural features blending well with more recent development.

ROWINGTON:
The scattered nature of Rowlington betrays its farming roots but it neverthe-less manages to retain a strong sense of community through its pub, church and cricket club.

SOLIHULL:
Known as 'the town in the country', Solihull retains a presence distinct from nearby Birmingham. Dating back to Saxon times, these days the town has a bright modern feel and benefits from excellent transport links.

> Solihull, and the area surrounding it, was the setting for Edith Holden's *Country Diary of an Edwardian Lady*.

SHREWLEY:
A small village just off the main road near the Shrewley Tunnel with its own stores and pub and a number of converted farm workers' buildings.

HISTORY

Much of the land covering this section was once occupied by the great Forest of Arden, hence the fact that many places in the area have the suffix 'in-Arden' appended to their name, although these days hardly anything remains of what was once a defining feature of the centre of the country.

Indeed, it is only in relatively recent times that the towns and villages to the north of the section have attained any real size, with Solihull in particular a late developer. As recently as a century ago, Solihull had only around 8,000 residents, the Industrial Revolution that had transformed Birmingham having passed the town by.

That said, Solihull is no new town and can trace its origins back to Norman times, although at the time of Domesday it was little more than a clearing in the forest where people came to trade. Tax records first date the town around 1180, when its position at the confluence of two medieval roads, combined with the presence of a holy well, led to the establishment of the church of St Alphege. In time, the spire of St Alphege came to dominate the High Street, although these days it is dwarfed by shops.

Before too long, Solihull, which gained its name from the 'soly' (meaning miry or muddy) hill of red marl that distinguished the area, had become more important than the older Anglo-Saxon settlement of Ulverlei to the north west, which began to be known as Old Town, or in modern use, Olton.

Market rights were granted in 1242, and in 1417 Henry V claimed the manor as his own, but Solihull was destined to remain relatively unimportant for a

People living in Solihull are known as Silhillians, with old boys from the local grammar school known as Old Silhillians.

few centuries yet, its isolated position affording it some protection from outside influences, although it did gain something of a reputation for the manufacture of hunting weapons and agricultural equipment.

It took the founding of the railway in the nineteenth century to kick-start the growth of not only Solihull but also Knowle and Dorridge. The latter was first recorded around 1400, when it too became known as an open area in the surrounding forest, 'Derrech' meaning a 'clearing in the wood'. That was all it remained, though, with barely enough housing to even merit hamlet status.

Knowle was a little bigger, owing its existence to a position on slightly higher ground, as its name might also suggest. At the beginning of the fifteenth century a small community had built up here, and it was their plight that led to the building of a church by local man Walter Cook, as the residents had to otherwise walk 8 miles to Hampton-in-Arden, crossing the dangerous River Blythe en route.

It took a further 400 years for Knowle to become a parish in its own right, a period that coincided with the growth of Dorridge, which in turn brings this story back to the railway. In 1852, local landowner George Muntz agreed to let the Great Western Railway build its line through his lands at Widney Manor on the condition that a station was included at Dorridge to allow him to travel to London.

Catesby Lane in Lapworth is named after one-time resident William Catesby, father of the Gunpowder Plot conspirator, Robert. A more recent Lapworth celebrity is the comedian Jasper Carrott, or Bob Davis as his family know him.

This proved to be the making of both Knowle and Dorridge, the station adopting the names of both in 1899. The villages became popular commuter stops, a destiny that was also to befall Solihull and Lapworth further down the line.

Solihull's commuters were initially the more well to do, looking for somewhere more conducive than the industrial sprawl of Birmingham. The town became an administrative centre, holding its own Petty Sessions, and also had a Grammar School as well as a growing number of grand houses.

After the First World War growth really took off, with the population more than doubling in the 1930s. Further growth followed the establishment of a factory for Land Rover, and in the 1960s the historic High Street, comprising mainly Victorian terraced houses, made way for the Mell Square development. Growth continued, with the town gaining Metropolitan Borough status in 1974, and in the late 1980s, plans were laid to further develop the centre, plans which eventually came to fruition with the Touchwood development in 2001.

Solihull Grammar School is notorious for once rejecting an application from Samuel Johnson to become its headmaster.

Around the same time, Dorridge was earmarked for massive development as part of what was known as the 'Four Ashes Triangle', a process which has boosted the population by around 20,000 and allowed Dorridge to retain an identity separate from nearby Knowle.

These days the area as a whole benefits from its proximity not only to the railway, but to the more modern transport hubs that are the airport, along with the M42 and its junction with the M40. The National Exhibition Centre just off the M42 is also nearby. Meanwhile, the villages to the south of the section, over the border in Warwickshire, have similarly managed to retain some independence from the presence of Warwick and Leamington Spa, whose story will feature more prominently in the following section.

THE NATURAL LANDSCAPE

The River Blythe separates Solihull from Knowle, although it is the motorway which has adopted its valley that provides a more effective barrier now. The landscape along this stretch is fairly flat, as the evidence of only five locks along its length testifies. Small brooks are scattered around the fields that characterise the view further south, with woodland at a premium. The most notable exception to this is Hay Wood, north of Rowington, an ancient woodland managed by the Forestry Commission.

ACCESS AND TRANSPORT

ROADS

The M42 cuts a path through Solihull and Knowle to the north of this section, while the M40 (which it meets at Junction 3A) cuts a diagonal path from the north west to south east, encountering the canal near to Shrewley. The main trunk road is the A4141 which passes down from Solihull, through Knowle and Chadwick End and on to Five Ways, where it meets up with the A4177, which takes up the mantle of following a route slightly north of the towpath at this point. Elsewhere, a network of minor roads links up the other settlements along this section.

Knowle's Millennium sign.

RAIL

This stretch is well served with rail links, with five stations located at Solihull, Dorridge, Kingswood, Lapworth and Hatton. Trains linking these stops run along the Chiltern Railway line between Birmingham Snow Hill and Marylebone, while commuter trains also run from Solihull into Birmingham (Central Trains), and cross-country trains run by Virgin Trains link the town to Worcester.

Train operators serving this area are:
- Virgin Trains (08457 222333)
- Central Trains (0870 6096060)
- Chiltern Railways (08456 005165)

Otherwise, National Train Enquiries can be reached on 08457 484950.

BUSES

The following list sets out the main bus services on this section, although it is advisable to check before using them as some buses only run on certain days and others may have been withdrawn since publication of this Guide. It is also worth checking for more local services, in particular those linking districts of Solihull, where there are a number of circular and school-term-time only services.

- 40/41 – *Solihull to Dorridge (TWM)*
- 60 – *Solihull to Leamington Spa via Chadwick End, Lapworth and Rowington (A&M Group)*
- 151 – *Solihull to Dorridge (Claribel) – via Knowle (evenings and Saturdays only)*
- 197 – *Chadwick End, Knowle, Solihull (Claribel)*
- 514 – *Solihull, Knowle, Five Ways (A&M)*

Routes linking Solihull to Section A include:

- 4, 6, 57 – *Solihull to Birmingham (TWM)*
- 30 – *Solihull to Acocks Green (TWM)*

In addition, the National Express route 420 is a daily route linking Birmingham and London via Solihull.

Contact details for bus operators in this area are listed below, although Traveline (www.traveline.org.uk) on 0870 6082608 can give details of specific services between 7 a.m. and 10 p.m., and the Centro Transport Hotline (0121 200 2700) can also provide local information on bus services:

- A&M Group (01926 612487)
- Claribel (0121 7897878)
- National Express (08705 808080)
- TWM – Travel West Midlands (0121 2547272)

TAXIS

The following list gives a selection of the taxi operators in this section:

- 7-11 Radio Cars, Solihull (0121 711 7777)
- Angies Cars, Solihull (0121 707 1881)
- Crown Cars, Solihull (0121 687 1900)
- Gemini Cars, Dorridge (01564 230230)
- Go2 Cars, Solihull (0121 705 2222)
- Knowle Cars, Knowle (01564 777007)
- Knowle and Dorridge Cars, Knowle (01564 730200)

SECTION A   SALFORD JUNCTION TO CATHERINE DE BARNES

Top: *Birmingham Town Hall.*

Bottom: *Snow Hill Bridge.*

Opposite top: *Solihull Straight.*

Opposite bottom: *A bricked-up doorway for the old Great Western Railway at Snow Hill Station.*

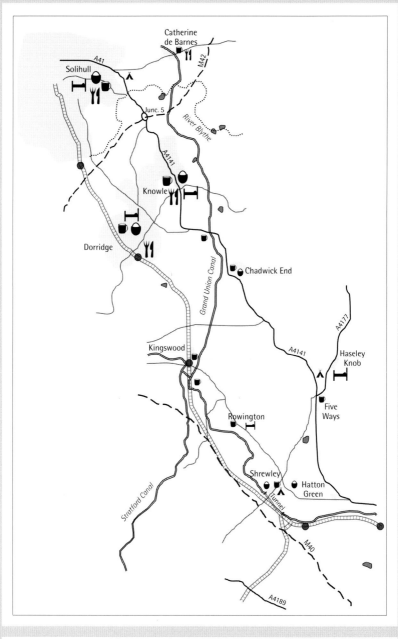

Key

═══	Canal	⬤ Built up area	⬤ Shops	
······	River	⬤ Stations	⊢ Accomodation	
▥▥▥	Railway	◗ Open water	⋀ Campsite	
─ ─ ─	Motorway		⬤ Pub	
────	A Road		⅄⅃ Restaurant	
────	B Road			

BASICS

INTRODUCTION

Between the two picturesque villages of Catherine de Barnes and Hatton Green lies the large town of Solihull, which retains a proud independence from Birmingham, in whose shadow it sits, and the two, similarly distinct, towns of Knowle and Dorridge. Each of these offers a diversity of shopping opportunities, while the growing number of villages that mark the beginning of Warwickshire are notable for their pubs, many of which sit on the canal.

There is also a Tourist Information Centre in Solihull Central Library (0121 704 6130).

SHOPPING

The abundance of shopping opportunities which started in the previous section continues as Birmingham subsides into Solihull, and in turn into Knowle and Dorridge before the rural hinterland of Warwickshire begins to take over. The latter offers opportunities to stock up on basic supplies while Solihull operates as a major centre and Knowle (more than Dorridge), more basic market-town-type shops.

Solihull is a busy modern centre basically broken down into three parts: a pedestrianised High Street and two more formal shopping centres, Mell Square and Touchwood. Most of the smaller independent stores are along the High Street, while the Mell Square Centre is sandwiched between the High Street and Warwick Road, and has over ninety stores in an open-air environment, including a Morrisons and a Sainsbury's supermarket. Mell Square also boasts a Beatties and a Marks & Spencer as well as other familiar names such as Boots. Drury Lane within Mell Square is also good for independent stores.

The Touchwood development was opened in 2001 and has three arcades, each with their own 'feel': Poplar, Crescent and Mill Lane. Touchwood also hosts the town's cinema and has a number of eateries which means that it continues to buzz outside of normal shopping hours. For many, Touchwood's most distinguishing feature is the fact that it houses the only John Lewis in the West Midlands. Finally, there is a Farmer's Market in the High Street on the first Friday of each month.

Haycock Farm, just off the towpath.

SECTION A   SALFORD JUNCTION TO CATHERINE DE BARNES

Top: *The view out towards Camp Hill.*

Bottom: *Skirting Aston*

Opposite top: *Birmingham's magnificent Town Hall.*

Opposite bottom: *Looking down from Snow Hill Bridge..*

Slightly to the east of Solihull on the canal sits Catherine de Barnes, where there is a convenience store, newsagent and post office all in one. There are also a couple of organic farm shops: Oak Farm (0121 705 5155) and the Hopwood (0121 711 7787).

Knowle is a good market town clustered around a compact centre, with good basic shops and services, including a Tesco Metro, a Gourmet Delicatessen and the Knowle Shopping Centre with a number of more local stores. Just outside the town there is also Happy Hens free range eggs (01564 772958). Dorridge also has a Tesco Express and two parades of local shops, with one built around three sides of a square.

Both Chadwick End and Hatton Green have post offices, with the latter also having a village stores and the former a farm shop just on its outskirts. Finally, there are also some basic shops in Shrewley.

EATING AND DRINKING

There is a good selection of towpath pubs as well as others scattered in the surrounding villages along this stretch, with Solihull slightly disappointing as a drinking destination.

- The Boat Inn, Catherine de Barnes (0121 7050474)
- Barley Mow, Solihull (0121 711 3761)
- The Coach House, Solihull (0121 709 0946)
- Hogshead, Solihull (0121 711 3630)
- The Masons Arms, Solihull (0121 711 8041)
- The Red House, Solihull (0121 711 8856)
- The Saddlers Arms, Solihull (0121 711 8001)
- The Heron's Nest near Knowle (01564 771177) – *by Bridge 70*
- The Red Lion, Knowle (01564 771522)
- The Vaults, Knowle (01564 773656) – *real ale bar*
- The Wilsons Arms, Knowle (01564 772559)
- The Black Boy, outside Knowle (01564 772655)
- The Drum and Monkey, Dorridge (01564 772242)
- The Railway, Dorridge (01564 773531)
- The Orange Tree. Chadwick End (01564 785364)
- The Navigation, Kingswood (01564 783337)
- The Case Is Altered, Five Ways (01926 484206)
- The Cock Horse, Rowington (01926 842183)
- Tom O'The Wood, Rowington (01564 782252)
- Durham Ox, Shrewley (01926 842283) – *restaurant and country pub*

A patron of the Tom O'Bedlam, which once served beer to the locals of Chadwick End, is said to have accused a fellow drinker of being an escaped lunatic from a nearby asylum, only to be told, 'no I am not and I have a certificate to prove it', a boast few people can match.

As befits its size, Solihull acts as the main focus for eating out in this section, and the following list offers a selection of restaurants in the town, many of which are congregated in the Touchwood entertainment complex:

- Beau Thai, Old Lode Lane
  (0121 743 5355) – *Thai*
- Harry Ramsdens, Touchwood
  (0121 709 1807) – *fish and chips*
- La Tasca, Touchwood
  (0121 709 1846) – *Spanish*
- Metro Bar and Grill, Warwick Road
  (0121 711 8030) – *traditional*
- Must, Touchwood (0121 711 8822)
  – *Chinese*
- Nandos, Touchwood (0121 711 2505)
  – *Portuguese*
- Pizza by Goli, Solihull ice rink
  (0121 743 3222) – *Italian*
- Tiggis, Touchwood (0121 713 2000)
  – *Italian*
- Townhouse Restaurant and Bar,
  Warwick Road (0121 704 1567)
  – *traditional*
- Yellow River Café, Touchwood
  (0121 711 6969) – *Chinese*

SECTION B

Elsewhere, both Knowle and Dorridge have something to offer, with a heavy emphasis on the Asian and Oriental cuisines, while Catherine de Barnes on the edge of Solihull also has its own restaurant:

- Longfellows Restaurant, Catherine
  de Barnes (0121 705 0587)
- The Bilash, Knowle (01564 773030)
  – *Indian*
- Café Saffron, Knowle
  (01564 772190) – *Indian*
- The Ellora, Knowle (01564 776400)
  – *Indian*
- The Gresweld Brasserie, Knowle
  (01564 772711)
- Knowle Indian Brasserie
  (01564 776453)
- Loch Fyne's Seafood, Knowle
  (01564 732750)
- Napoletana, Knowle (01564 779802)
  – *Italian*
- Phonlik House, Knowle
  (01564 775554) – *Chinese*
- Spirals Restaurant, Knowle
  (01564 739395)
- The Thai Village, Knowle
  (01564 771595)
- Tom Li, Knowle (01564 770824)
  – *Chinese*
- Da Santino, Dorridge
  (01564 772547) – *Italian*
- Minh's Cantonese, Dorridge
  (01564 779929) – *Chinese*
- Saleem Bagh, Dorridge
  (01564 777190) – *Indian*

Snacks and fast food are also easy to get hold of along this stretch, with the following a selection of what is available:

- Casa Bar and Restaurant,
  Touchwood, Solihull
  (0121 711 8881)
- Coffee Roaster, High Street, Solihull
  (0121 744 2735)
- Dorridge Cantonese, Dorridge
  (01564 774660) – *Chinese takeaway*
- Dorridge Fish Bar, Dorridge
  (01564 775954) – *fish and chips*
- Dragonfly Tea Rooms, Warwick
  Road, Solihull (0121 703 0846)
- Drucker's Vienna Patisserie,
  Touchwood, Solihull
  (0121 705 8957)
- Greedy Guts, Knowle (01564
  779240) – *sandwiches*
- The Knowle Fish Bar
  (01564 772739) – *fish and chips*
- O'Briens Irish Sandwich Bar,
  Touchwood, Solihull
  (0121 704 2622)

There is also a café bar attached to the Arts Centre next to the library in Solihull.

SECTION B   CATHERINE DE BARNES TO HATTON GREEN

Top: *The Heron's Nest near Knowle.*

Bottom: *Knowle Locks.*

Opposite top: *Knowle Top Lock.*

Opposite bottom: *Knowle's Almshouses.*

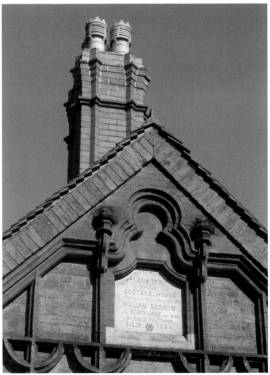

SLEEPING

There is a reasonable selection of places to stay along this stretch, although hotels in Solihull tend towards the large and modern, with half an eye on trade from Birmingham Airport, while the smaller and more intimate hotels tend to be more towards Knowle and Dorridge. There is also a free hotel bed booking service available on 0121 202 5005.

SECTION B

HOTELS

- Holiday Inn, Solihull (0121 623 9988) – *115-room modern hotel*
- Ramada, Solihull (0121 711 2121) – *145-room modern hotel*
- Renaissance Hotel, Solihull (0121 711 3000)

- The Greswolde Arms Hotel, Knowle (01564 772711) – *thirty-one rooms in the heart of Solihull*
- The Forest, Dorridge (01564 772120) – *twelve-room hotel with bar*
- Moat Manor Hotel, Dorridge (01564 779988) – *exclusive eight-room hotel set in own gardens*

BED AND BREAKFAST/GUEST HOUSES

There is also a good range of more modest accommodation along this stretch, although Solihull tends to offer less fertile territory.

- Leaded Light, Solihull (0121 707 8408)
- Oatlands, Solihull (0121 709 0347)
- Ravenhurst Guest House, Solihull (0121 704 0717)
- Achill Guest House, Knowle (01564 774090)
- The Heron's Nest near Knowle (01564 771177) – *by Bridge 70*
- Heronbrook Cottage, Knowle (01564 778157)

- Woodyard Cottage, Dorridge (01564 775420)
- The Croft Guest House, Haseley Knob (01926 484447)
- Shepherd's Fold Guest House, Haseley Hall Farm, Haseley (01926 484573)
- Shrewley Pools Farm, Haseley (01926 484315) – *working farm*
- Whitley Elm Cottages, Rowington (01926 4845777)

CAMPING

Campers are reasonably well catered for along this stretch of the towpath, with three sites within easy reach:

- Croft Caravan Site, Haseley Knob (01926 484447)
- Pitts Farm, Shrewley (01926 842737) – *five pitches in a*

two-acre field on a medieval farm with canal nearby
- Solihull Camp Site, Solihull (01676 533892) – *five pitches*

The nearest camping supplies outlets in this section are:

- Army and Navy Stores, Poplar Way, Solihull (0121 709 1951)
- Milletts, Drury Lane, Solihull (0121 711 3817)

- Oswald Bailey, Station Road, Solihull (0121 705 3226)
- Midwest Camping, Warwick Road, Knowle (01564 777972)

The southern portal of Shrewley Tunnel.

SECTION B   CATHERINE DE BARNES TO HATTON GREEN

Top: *Lapworth offers a choice of routes.*
Bottom: *Lapworth Arm Bridge.*

Top: *Knowle House.*
Bottom: *An unusual iron footbridge at Lapworth.*

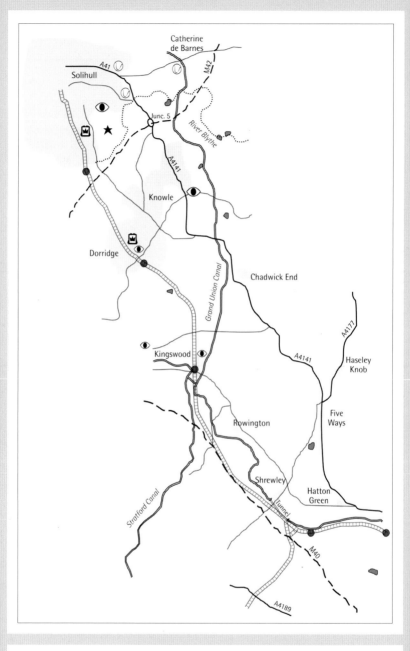

Key

═══	Canal	⬤	Built up area	◉	Site/Sight
··········	River	⬤	Stations	⊘	Leisure
▭▭▭	Railway	🪨	Open water	★	Entertainment
− − −	Motorway			🏛	Culture
───	A Road				
───	B Road				

SEEING AND DOING

INTRODUCTION

The relatively recent growth of the main towns along this stretch means that historical sights tend to be thin on the ground, although a few gems remain if you know where to look. What the area lacks in tradition, it more than makes up for with more modern, packaged, entertainment, although care has been taken in Solihull in particular to retain open spaces of parkland, catering for interests across the spectrum, from skateboarding to simply admiring the gardens.

SECTION B

SIGHTS

The main point of historical interest in Solihull, quite literally, is the church of St Alphege, which dates back to the late thirteenth century and has a fine spire that once dominated the High Street.

The oldest part of the church is the chancel, the most significant feature of which is the great east window, which, along with other windows in the church, has an unusual detail of double cusps. Look out also for the Crypt Chapel of All Souls, a rare medieval chapel in an undercroft with a stone rib-vault. Unusually, the steps to the altar are made of coal, which gives a highly polished appearance.

The only other landmarks of any real historical significance in Solihull are the old George Hotel which dates back to the sixteenth century and lives on today under the guise of the Ramada Jarvis, and the Manor House on the opposite side of the High Street, which dates back to 1495 and was built by the Greswold family.

The parish church in Knowle also acts as something of a focal point. Dedicated to St John the Baptist, St Lawrence the Martyr and St Anne, this was completed in 1403 and was built by local man made good, Walter Cook, on land owned by his parents.

> The consecration certificate for Knowle's church gives the date 'Anno domini one thousand CCCC and two', but subsequent changes in the calendar mean it was actually consecrated on 24 February 1403, meaning it celebrated its 600th anniversary in 2003.

The church is worth a visit, not least for its original font and the fifteenth-century wooden screen at the eastern end of the nave. The more modern pulpit also houses an hourglass thought to date from the seventeenth century, which was no doubt useful to keep a track on the length of sermons.

Next to the church is Knowle's Guild House. This dates back to the origins of the church, and was built for the Guild of St Anne, a religious charity which was dissolved during the Reformation. The house was eventually donated to the church by the then owner, a Mr Jackson, in 1912, along with St Anne's Cottage.

Close to the Guild House is Chester House (01564 775840), a good example of an Elizabethan town house which is now used as the local library. The house dates back to 1400 and is particularly notable for its knot garden at the back.

SECTION C   HATTON TO LONG ITCHINGTON

Top left: *Offchurch Millennium window.*

Top right: *Cubbington Sign.*

Bottom: *Leamington Spa, Jephson Gardens entrance.*

Opposite top: *Warwick Eastgate.*

Opposite bottom: *Hatton Locks.*

Guided tours are available in the summer (not Wednesdays) and entrance is free.

An amble down the High Street in Knowle will reward the sharp-eyed as there are a number of historic buildings. These include the Berrow Homes which stand on what was once the village green and have their own stocks, and the Red Lion, one of four pubs that used to stand on the Warwick Turnpike (now the A41) through the town. In addition, there is a smattering of sixteenth- and seventeenth-century cottages, many of which now operate as businesses, and it is worth glancing up away from the shop fronts to gain a full appreciation of the town's history.

> Sitting in a triangle between Starbold Crescent, Landor Road and Hillmorton Road, near the park is a small nature reserve, an area wrestled free from developers by a determined group of locals in the 1970s. Purnells Brook, a tributary of the River Blythe, adds to the tranquillity of the scene.

Nearby Dorridge is less blessed with older buildings, but has one or two oddities worth consideration. One of these is the Dorridge Grove on Knowle Wood Road. This was originally built in the mid-nineteenth century as an asylum for twenty 'idiot girls' and was so successful that it was replaced in 1872. In 1877 it was rebuilt as the 'Midland Counties Middleclass Idiots Asylum' and was supported by the local freemasons. Despite the use of the words 'idiot' and 'asylum', this was actually a rather prestigious institution where parents of academically challenged children would pay for remedial education.

> Until the invention of the moveable hive, bees were kept in skeps made of wicker or coiled straw, and in particularly exposed areas these would in turn be kept in recesses in walls known as 'bee boles'. Most were made to face the early morning sun to encourage the bees to start work early!

Outside of the main towns there are two National Trust properties in the area: Baddesley Clinton (01564 783294) south of Knowle, a fifteenth-century Elizabethan house with three priest holes and gardens featuring a stewpond, lakeside walk and nature trail, and Packwood House (also 01564 783294) near Lapworth, a Tudor manor house with good collections of stained glass and tapestries. The gardens are a particular feature here and include a walled area, a seventeenth-century Yew Garden representing the Sermon on the Mount and 'bee boles' in the wall of the Garden Terrace which date from 1756.

CULTURE AND ENTERTAINMENT

There is a good range of places to go to sustain the inner soul along this stretch, starting with the Solihull Art Gallery (0121 705 7838) which, despite its name, is situated in Catherine de Barnes. In Solihull itself there is the Solihull Arts Complex (0121 704 6962), a multi-arts venue in the middle of town next to the library. The centre has a 339-seat theatre, a gallery area and a multipurpose studio space, and has a varied programme ranging from films and tribute bands through to lectures and concerts featuring the likes of the Solihull Symphony Orchestra and the Midland Youth Jazz Orchestra. The Touchwood Centre, also in Solihull, has the area's main cinema, the Cineworld (0871 220 8000).

There are two leisure centres in this section, both in Solihull and on Blossomfield Road. The most significant of these is the Tudor Grange Centre

Bridge and lock at Lapworth.

(0121 705 6371) which has a 33m main pool and a diving pool, as well as Paradise Falls, a three-flume leisure pool. This also has a sports hall and health suite. The second is the Norman Green Sports Centre (0121 705 4474), based around an athletics track which is also home to the Solihull & Small Heath Athletics Club. The centre also has an AstroTurf pitch, gym and facilities for racket sports.

As has already been mentioned, Solihull is justly proud of its open spaces and is home to three of the West Midlands' ten 'Green Flag' parks. The Malvern and Brueton Park is a short walk away from the town centre and has tennis courts and a vivid display of bedding plants in the summer. It also has the Parkridge Centre, a conservation education centre run by the Warwickshire Wildlife Trust, as well as a secret garden with carved wooden sculptures.

The Tudor Grange Park, also close to the centre, has an eighteen-hole pitch and putt course, as well as places for skateboarding, BMXing and blading. Slightly out of town is Elmdon Park, which has the advantage of being a little higher and offers good views over the surrounding countryside, as well as what remains of the walled garden that once belonged to Elmdon Hall.

Finally, Catherine de Barnes hosts the Solihull Canoe Club (0121 745 3415) which caters for paddlers of all ages. It offers coaching and has a wildwater racing group.

SECTION C   HATTON TO LONG ITCHINGTON

Top: *Leamington Spa boulevard.*
Bottom: *Leycester Hospital, Warwick.*

Opposite top: *All Saints Church, Leamington Spa.*
Opposite bottom: *A traditional bandstand in Leamington Spa.*

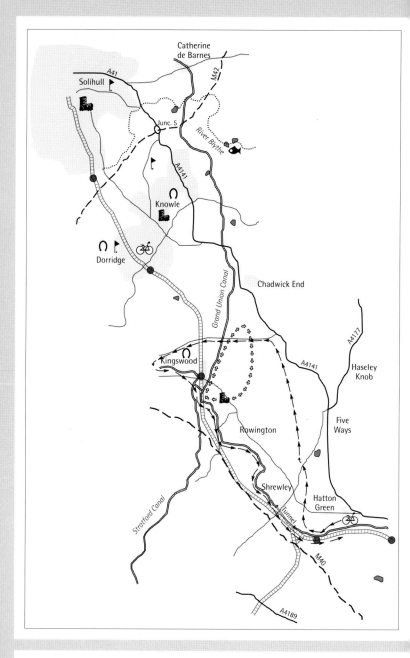

Key

Canal	Built up area	Cycling route/outlet
River	Stations	Walking route/outlet
Railway	Open water	Fishing spot/outlet
Motorway		Golf course/outlet
A Road		Riding outlet
B Road		

SAMPLING

INTRODUCTION

This is a section of contrasts, with the large modern development of Solihull to the north and Knowle and Dorridge offering a smaller version of the same just below, followed by large open areas of farmland to the south and east. Kingswood Junction acts as a significant crossroads on the canal system and has the convenience of car parks and pubs which makes it a natural focus for either some formal sampling of the area or merely some gentle gongoozling. The section is covered by OS Explorer Maps 220 Birmingham and 221 Coventry and Warwick.

WALKING

Other than the canal, there are two formal walking routes through this section. The first of these is the Solihull Way, a 17.5-mile route linking Earlswood Lakes and the Stratford Canal in the south to Castle Bromwich Gardens in the north. Both these points are outside the area covered in this section, although the path describes a route through the centre of Solihull heading south-west using mainly well-defined roads and tracks.

The second path is the Heart of England Way, a 100-mile route that cuts across the West Midlands, joining Cannock Chase in Staffordshire with the Cotswolds. As far as this section is concerned, the path cuts across the A41 at Chadwick End, passes through Baddesley Clinton (part of the route is utilised in Walk B on page 76), through Rowington and across the towpath before following the line of the Stratford Canal south after Kingswood Junction.

As well as these routes, there is also the ancient woodland of Hay Wood north of Baddesley Clinton, which is managed by the Forestry Commission and has its own car park as well as a good range of wildlife. Dorridge Park is also worth a visit. All that remains of a 50-acre wood first mentioned in 1556, this ancient woodland includes scots pine, oak, ash, wych elm, sycamore and beech, which provide a good habitat for wildlife such as foxes, owls and voles, as well as wildflowers such as dogs mercury and wood sorrel.

Walk B starts at Kingswood and is a short stroll taking in both the canal and parts of the surrounding countryside.

Catherine de Barnes.

SECTION D   LONG ITCHINGTON TO NORTON JUNCTION

Top: *Stockton Locks.*

Bottom: *A colourful Butty in Braunston.*

Opposite top: *Long Itchingdon.*

Opposite bottom: *Braunston, on the hill above the canal.*

SECTION B WALK
Kingswood and back via Baddesley Clinton

Description:	*An easy stroll with only gentle gradients, with many of the footpaths solid tracks.*
Distance:	*3.5 miles*
Duration:	*1.5 hours*
Starting point:	*Grid Reference 191709, OS Explorer 220 (South). Explorer 221 also required.*
Nearest refreshment:	*The Navigation, Kingswood*

Start from the Navigation Inn on the Old Warwick Road and join the canal towpath heading north as far as Bridge 66 (Rising Lane), which you cross. Pick up the footpath immediately on your left, heading north-east and then east after a field boundary. On reaching the road, turn left and pick up the path, which is in fact more of a track, on the other side after a couple of hundred yards.

Stay with the track as it heads south and converges with a more conventional path heading south. This meets Rising Lane once again where you turn right and then immediately left down Hay Wood Lane. Follow this for 300 yards until you find a path to the right on the corner of a field. Follow this slightly downhill, past a house on your left and along the edge of some trees. You are now on the Heart of England Way which is well signposted.

Stick with the path as it skirts to the north of Baddesley Clinton and cuts across some fields. This eventually comes out onto another track where you head left (south), past the farm and out onto a road where you turn right and back to the pub.

Walking equipment outlets along this section include:

- Midwest Camping, Wyndley Garden Centre, Knowle (01564 777972)
- Millets, Solihull (0121 711 3817)
- Oswald Bailey, Solihull (0121 705 3226)

Lapworth Arm.

Lapworth.

CYCLING

The flat terrain and plethora of country roads to the south of this stretch mean it is possible to put together some decent rides, although the more built-up area around Solihull and Knowle is less good. That said, the Solihull Way is cycle-friendly and ends at Earlswood Lakes, just south-west of the Stratford Canal.

A recommended route begins at the top of the Hatton Locks, where there is some convenient parking, and follows the towpath west as far as Bridge 56, where you turn right, over the bridge, and into Little Shrewley, crossing the B4439. Continue north, turning left at a T-junction, where you assume a north-westerly direction. Follow this through Mousely End, after which the road becomes Quarry Lane and then Hay Wood Lane, until you reach Rising Lane at a T-junction, where you head right (west).

Cross over the canal at Bridge 66 until you reach another T-junction, where you head left (south) until you reach the Stratford Canal. Follow the towpath left, along the Lapworth Flight, heading left again at the junction after Lock 19, following the link to the Grand Union where you turn right and head south, back to your starting point via the Shrewley Tunnel, over which you pass. This is a total of around 15 miles.

Cycle outlets along this section include:
• Dorridge Cycles (01564 779996)

RIDING

Formal bridleways are thin on the ground in this section. There is a short route linking Rowington and High Cross and an even shorter path to the east of Haseley Green, and the option to utilise parts of the Heart of England Way, but

SECTION D   LONG ITCHINGTON TO NORTON JUNCTION

Opposite top: *Braunston windmill.*

Opposite bottom: *Braunston Turn.*

Top: *Bridge 8, looking west.*

Bottom: *Braunston marina crane.*

otherwise riders are probably best advised to head to one of the establishments listed below. The Solihull Riding Club has particularly impressive facilities.

Horse-riding establishments and outlets along this section include:

- Heronfield Riding Stables, Knowle (01564 773406)
- Solihull Riding Club, Four Ashes, Dorridge (01564 770180) – *full-sized indoor arena and an all weather arena set on 220 acres with cross-country fences*
- Swallowfield Equestrian, Lapworth (01564 784475) – *riding school and stables*

FISHING

Canal fishing tends to be controlled by a diverse group of small angling societies along this section, often responsible for very small stretches and hard to track down. For example, the Lode Mill Angling Syndicate (0121 243 4332) runs the stretch between Bridges 76 and 77, followed by private fishing after Bridge 75.

The Birmingham Area Civil Service Angling Society controls the section around Knowle Locks while the Massey Ferguson Angling Club controls the section after Bridge 67, and the Oriental Angling Club the short section after that up to Bridge 65. The SPAC (024 7625 1659) are responsible for the section around Bridge 63, and the Stratford-upon-Avon Angling Association the waters by the southern portal of Shrewley Tunnel.

The casual angler may therefore be better off confining themselves to more formal waters. A good place to head is Blythe Waters, controlled by British Waterways from its Lapworth office (01564 784634). This offers four lakes and a stretch of the River Blythe where carp, bream, tench and roach are available, along with silver bream, barbell and chub.

Another good alternative is the Tunnel Barn Farm Fishery in Shrewley (01926 842188), which is a complex of seven pools and 2.5 miles of the canal. Alternatively, it may be worth phoning the Solihull Angling Club (0121 603 2637) for more local information.

Surprisingly, fishing supplies are not that easy to come by along this stretch. The two nearest outlets are both in Shirley, slightly off the map:

- Solihull Angling Centre, Shirley (0121 733 7775)
- easytackle.com, Shirley (0121 744 1376)

OTHER

There are two golf clubs along this stretch, along with a municipal pitch and putt in the centre of Solihull and a driving range:

- Copt Heath Golf Club, nr. Knowle (01564 772650) – *18 holes, 6,517 yards*
- Four Ashes Golf Range, Dorridge (01564 779055) – *28-bay floodlit and covered driving range*
- Tudor Grange Pitch and Putt – *18-hole pitch and putt, 9-hole putting green*
- Widney Manor Golf Club (0121 711 3646) – *18 holes, 5,654 yards*

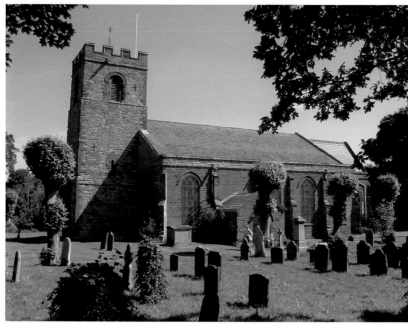

SECTION E   NORTON JUNCTION TO BLISWORTH

Top: *Blisworth cottages.*

Bottom: *Taking their thyme.*

Opposite top: *Bugbrooke.*

Opposite bottom: *Weedon church.*

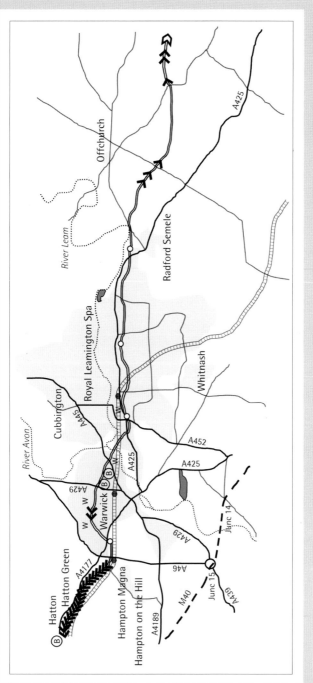

Key
- Canal
- River
- Railway
- Motorway
- A Road
- B Road
- Built up area
- Stations
- Open water
- Turning point
- Lock
- Boatyard
- Waterpoint

SHAPERS

THE CANAL ON THIS STRETCH

KEY FACTS

LENGTH: 12 miles

BOATYARDS: 4
  Stephen Goldsborough Boats, Hatton
  Saltisford Canal Centre, Warwick
  Kate Boats, Warwick
  Delta Marine Services, Warwick

WATERPOINTS: 4
  Above Cape Locks
  Below Cape Locks
  Kate Boats, Warwick
  Bridge 43

TURNING POINTS: 4
  Saltisford Arm Junction
  Bridge 38
  Bridge 43
  Radford Semele

LOCKS: 32
  Hatton Flight (21) (146ft 6in)
  Cape Locks (2) (14ft 4in)
  Fosse Locks (3) (21ft)
  Wood Lock (6ft 7in)
  Welsh Road Lock (6ft 11in)
  Bascote Locks (4) (26ft 9in)

Although passing through the urban combination of Warwick and Leamington Spa, this stretch is enlivened by the Hatton Locks to the west and a rural section to the east which ends with a staircase lock. The towpath is bumpy in places, but is generally good.

Between Hatton station and Bridge 55, the towpath improves in terms of firmness, but deteriorates sharply in terms of evenness, becoming really quite bumpy. There is a turning point along this straight stretch and matters pick up after the bridge and the run up to the locks, just before which there is a run of moorings ending in a small café.

The long, twenty-one-lock Hatton flight now begins, with the locks evenly spaced for most of the length, creating quite a spectacular sight from the top.

SECTION E NORTON JUNCTION TO BLISWORTH

Top: *Bugbroke.*

Bottom: *Norton Junction.*

Opposite top: *Bridge 47, a turnover bridge.*

Opposite bottom: *Blisworth.*

This is a favourite spot for visitors and there is a parking area just off the A4177, south of Hatton village, opposite some BW buildings.

The towpath is in very good condition here, passing over to the left at Bridge 54 after the fourth lock. Bridge 52 is somewhat unfairly known as Ugly Bridge (there are a lot that are worse!), and after it the locks continue but have longer gaps between them. The canal also takes a slight list to the right, following the line of the (unseen for now) railway. The surrounding landscape remains distinctly rural here.

> The Hatton Locks were reopened in 1934 by the then Duke of Kent – the completion of an ambitious project to widen all the locks between Napton and Birmingham to allow the passage of 14ft-wide barges and thus improve the efficiency of the canal.

The canal turns sharp left at the entrance to the Saltisford Arm, although a huge sign welcoming boats to the waterway may make it easy to go wrong. Aim to pass under the modern road bridge, the first of many bridges which gives away the fact that you are now entering the first significant built-up area since Birmingham.

The rural tranquillity of the last few miles now gives way to the steady encroachment of Warwick, which begins unpromisingly with the local cemetery on the left. A run of visitors' moorings follows at Cape, and if you thought the locks were over, there is a further pair here by a pub. Water points exist either side of the locks.

> The Saltisford Arm is all that remains of the Warwick terminus of the Warwick & Birmingham Canal. It was restored from dereliction between 1982 and 1988 by the Saltisford Canal Trust, from whom it is possible to hire temporary moorings or their self-steer 32ft-boat *Saltie* (01926 490006).

New housing begins to make its mark on the landscape on both banks, as the canal curves to the right just before Bridge 49. Immediately afterwards there is the Kate Boats boatyard and a long run of ringed visitors' moorings, opposite which there is the working Delta Marine Services boatyard.

The canal passes round the edge of the centre of Warwick, but to the east, at Bridge 46, there is a useful Tesco with its own moorings. The canal passes over the River Avon – the de facto border between Warwick and Leamington Spa, via an aqueduct, followed shortly by another after Bridge 45 carrying the canal over the railway. After Bridge 44 there is a swing to the left and more housing where the towpath diverts round a winding hole.

There are some moorings outside the appropriately named Mooring pub adjacent to Bridge 43, with the Tiller Pin on the opposite bank offering an alternative. You are now firmly in Leamington Spa, where the A425 comes alongside for a while before the canal dips into a tree-lined cutting which ends with a curve to the right at Bridge 41, where there is access to the station.

A long, straight section then follows with town houses and ringed moorings. These are joined by less than attractive commercial buildings which turn their backs on the canal. There is a winding hole just after Bridge 38 and a half-mile straight stretch follows Bridge 37. The Radford Road Bridge (No.5) marks the eastern limit of Leamington, after which the canal pulls to the right. The tower of Radford Semele church is visible in a clearing to the right.

A weir into the River Leam appears just before another winding hole, with the river itself flowing below and to the left for a short while. The towpath remains solid immediately outside Leamington and there are plenty of mooring opportunities along this stretch. Bridge 34 marks the beginning of five evenly spaced locks, with an imposing railway viaduct after the first of these making for an impressive sight.

The towpath bends away to the left after the second lock and begins to deteriorate significantly in quality. The landscape becomes distinctly rural around here and, perhaps out of sympathy, the towpath soon grasses over completely.

A sanitary station appears just before Bridge 32 and a run of permanent moorings occupies Fosse Wharf before the last of the five locks. After this, the canal curves gently to the left and then right again before opening out into a short straight that leads you up to Bridge 29 and the beginning of the four Bascote Locks, the last two of which are a staircase.

> Bricks along this section of the Grand Union were some of the 3 million made locally in the winter of 1795. The clay was dug in Offchurch and baked in a kiln at Radford.

The quality of the towpath improves immeasurably around here, albeit temporarily. Another long, slow sweep to the left follows the excitement of the staircase, with another sanitary and waterpoint on the apex of the curve. This ends with a railway bridge where the canal leans to the right, passing over an aqueduct just before Bridge 26, with the following bridge marking the main road passing through Long Itchington.

PRINCIPAL TOWNS AND VILLAGES ALONG THIS STRETCH

CUBBINGTON:
The older part of Cubbington is the meat in the sandwich between the Kings Head and the Queen's Head, while the newer quarter is a sprawl of modern housing.

> The nickname for someone from Cubbington is an 'ear biter', a name bestowed after a football match in which a player's ear was bitten off.

HAMPTON ON THE HILL:
As its name suggests, this small hamlet sits slightly higher than its namesake and is little more than farms and some more recent building.

HAMPTON MAGNA:
Sitting in the shadow of the new Warwick Parkway railway station, Hampton Magna consists mainly of modern semi-detached housing set back from the road, and has little to recommend itself to the casual visitor.

HATTON:
The scene of rapid growth, especially around the Hatton Park area, which is almost new town-like in appearance, with a profusion of anonymous estates punctuated with roundabouts. Otherwise, Hatton is its locks.

HATTON GREEN:
Hatton Green retains some of the charm that once might have been in Hatton itself, with a cluster of housing just off the main road.

SECTION F   STOKE BRUERNE TO MILTON KEYNES (NORTH)

Top: *A pair moving along the Great Ouse Aqueduct.*

Bottom: *Stoke Bruerne, Boat Inn.*

Opposite top: *Stoke Bruerne.*

Opposite bottom: *The Great Ouse or Wolverton Aqueduct from above.*

OFFCHURCH:

This dispersed village takes its name from the Saxon King Offa of Mercia, who is thought to have been buried here. The church and hall in the centre offer a clear centre, with other housing spreading down from a hill.

RADFORD SEMELE:

Straddling the A425 on the side of a hill, Radford Semele offers a mix of half timbered and thatched housing alongside more modern estates, with the latter merging effortlessly into the periphery of Leamington Spa.

> Although it is difficult to appreciate it from the towpath, Radford is quite close to the canal and even has a lock named after it.

ROYAL LEAMINGTON SPA:

Split in two by the River Leam, from which it takes its name and from whose floods it periodically suffers, the north is more elegant and is the centre for the Pump Rooms which confer the Spa suffix as well as the impressive Georgian Parade. Most modern development is in the form of congested new housing and vast industrial estates to the south.

WARWICK:

A compact town brimming with history and overlooked by its magnificent castle. Tudor and seventeenth-century buildings line the town centre streets with a range of interesting hotels and shops as well as a restaurant quarter.

> Leamington's most significant son was, without doubt, the onetime cobbler, postmaster and poet Benjamin Satchwell, who discovered the spring that transformed Leamington's fortunes and went on to found The Parade. These days he is more famous as the name of a popular pub.

WHITNASH:

With the exception of the occasional thatched cottage, Whitnash is a largely featureless suburb of housing on the outskirts of Leamington Spa.

HISTORY

Although Leamington is mentioned in the Domesday Book, as Lamintone, the main focus of historical interest in this section is Warwick. The town was founded on the banks of the River Avon in 914 when Ethelfleda, sister of the Mercian king Edward the Elder, shored up defences against the Viking invaders.

The Danes invaded Mercia 100 years later and the town was burned down, the first of two major conflagrations that have shaped the town's history. What remained of the defences led to the town becoming a regional centre. By the time of the conquest Warwick was a Royal Borough, and even had an established grammar school, which remains today.

Work on the castle began in 1068 after the Conquest, and it became the focus of attention both physically and administratively. By this time the town already had a population of around 1,500. Growth was slow, however, rising by just a third 500 years later.

The castle was built on the site of the original fortifications and was modelled on the standard Norman motte and bailey design. In 1264 it was sacked by Simon de Montfort, who ransomed the then Earl of Warwick. Ownership subsequently passed to the Beauchamp family, who added most of the features visible today. The castle remained in the family's ownership until 1978 when it was sold to the Tussaud Group, whose influence is clear.

> Warwick School is the third oldest surviving school in the country with claims to having been chartered by Edward the Confessor, and stronger evidence of being re-founded by Henry VIII.

The second major fire took place in 1694, destroying most of the centre and leading to the reconstruction of the town in the elegant Queen Anne and George I style, which now sit well with the medieval structures that survived. One such survivor was the Beauchamp Chapel in the church of St Mary's, which contains a full-sized reclining copper gilt effigy of Richard Beauchamp, Earl of Warwick, on Purbeck marble dating from 1459. From the late 1700s onwards Warwick began to be overshadowed by Leamington, and although the two have remained distinct towns, the dividing line between them can be confusing.

As has already been mentioned, Leamington existed at the time of the conquest but at that time was little more than a hamlet. For the 400 years before the beginning of the 1800s it was known as Leamington Priors, and existed mainly on the land south of the Leam. Before that it had belonged to the Priors of Kenilworth.

That the town was the source of mineral water was known in the Middle Ages, but this knowledge seemed to excite little local interest. The original spring lay in front of the parish church on land belonging to the Earl of Aylesford, the local lord. He saw little value in it and it took some enterprising locals, encouraged by the success of Bath and Harrogate, to come together to find a second source, which they did on one of their member's land in 1784. The owner, William Abbotts, had been working with Benjamin Satchell and together they built Abbott's 'Original' baths in Bath Lane (now Bath Street) two years later.

After twenty-five years of struggling to cope with growing numbers of visitors, a company was formed to buy land to the north of the Leam and develop a new bath complex, and the 'new town' of Leamington was born. The complex opened in 1814 and claimed to offer cures for 'stiffness of tendons' and the effects of gout, as well as acting as a laxative.

The town's reputation was aided by a visit from Princess Victoria in 1830, leading eight years later to the granting of the right to add the prefix 'Royal' to the town's name.

Leamington's popularity began to wane; by the middle of the century the fashion for 'taking the waters' had passed and in 1860 the Pump Rooms were sold as development land. A series of ill-advised schemes followed until 1996 when lottery money allowed the rooms to reopen as today's museum, art gallery and tourist centre. During that time the town had grown as a shopping centre, attracting retired people and commuters from Birmingham, and today the town exists as a regional centre and has large industrial estates to the south.

Whitnash also has a brief mention in the Domesday Book, as Witenas, although its stronger claim to fame is probably as the junction of a number of leylines passing through it. The main Roman Road from Radford Semele to Whitnash also passes through Whitnash Brook Valley, the original site of the village.

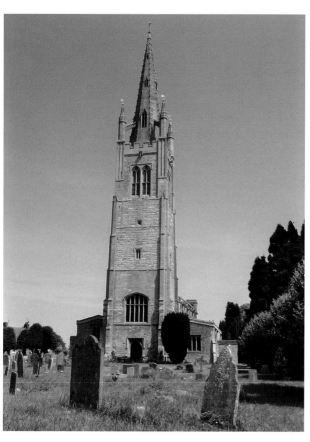

SECTION F   STOKE BRUERNE TO MILTON KEYNES (NORTH)

Top: *Boats on Tove Junction.*

Bottom: *Grafton Regis in the distance.*

Opposite top: *Hanslope church.*

Opposite bottom: *Cosgrove Bridge.*

Despite these antecedents, Whitnash remained relatively cut off through succeeding centuries and was only reconnected with a road to surrounding areas in the mid-nineteenth century, a fact many connect with the village's strong sense of independence – even today the town council remains strongly non-party political.

Of the local villages, Offchurch has the most noble history. It derives its name from Offa, King of Mercia in the mid-700s, who may have had a fort near the village, probably near the site of the present Manor House, the Bury, 'bury' being itself derived from 'berig', the Saxon for 'fortified place'.

Legend has it that Offa had a son called Fremund, who was murdered near Long Itchington and was subsequently buried at Offchurch. As some venerated him as a saint, this added to the church's importance. After the Norman Conquest the village passed to Coventry Abbey, passing in turn on the dissolution to Sir Edmund Knightly of Fawsley, whose family kept it until 1911.

THE NATURAL LANDSCAPE

SECTION C

The River Leam defines much of the landscape to the east of this section, joining from the north and winding its way past Offchurch before widening out into its full glory in Leamington Spa and flowing into the Avon at the meeting point between that town and Warwick. Although the Avon flows away to the south, its valley is a dramatic feature on the local landscape, one bridged by both the canal and the railway.

The Hatton Flight offers equally dramatic evidence of the higher ground to the west of the section, and to a lesser degree to the east, with the Avon Valley again exerting its influence. The land either side of the two towns is open and rural, although woodland is sparse with the exception of the woodlands south of Warwick.

ACCESS AND TRANSPORT

ROADS

The M40 cuts a section off the western corner of the section, with Junction 15 providing convenient access to Warwick. Elsewhere, the A425 is the main route to the east, passing into Leamington and onto and out of Warwick before heading south. The A455 heads out north-east from Warwick and the A429 cuts a north–south route through the town.

The A46 acts as the main trunk road to the west, skirting Warwick and joining up with the motorway, while the A4177 picks up the mantle of the A425 and acts as the main road heading west to Hatton.

Of the minor roads, the Fosse Way Roman Road crosses the canal at Bridge 32 and passes to the east of Offchurch, while Whitnash is connected to Leamington via the significant B8047.

RAIL

There are three stations in this section, all on the same line: Warwick Parkway, Warwick and Leamington Spa, the latter's art-deco design offering a contrast to the modernity of the Parkway. Central's trains terminate in Leamington Spa, which also has trains running through it operated by Virgin Cross Country, linking Leamington to Coventry, and points north as well as to Oxford and Reading, and points south. Otherwise, the main operator is Chiltern Railways operating their Birmingham to London Marylebone service.

Train operators serving this area are listed in Section B. Otherwise, National Train Enquiries can be reached on 08457 484950.

BUSES

The following list sets out the main bus services in this section, although it is advisable to check before using them as some buses only run on certain days and others may have been withdrawn since publication of this Guide. It is also worth checking for more local services, in particular those linking districts of Warwick and Leamington, where there are a number of circular and school-term-time only services.

- 16 – *Warwick to Leamington (SMR)*
- 18 – *Warwick to Leamington (SMR)*
- 60 – *Hatton to Leamington via Warwick (A&M)*
- 63 – *Leamington Spa to Radford Semele (SMR)*
- 66 – *Warwick to Whitnash via Leamington (SMR)*
- 68 – *Leamington Spa to Cubbington (SMR)*
- 75 – *Leamington to Hatton Park via Warwick and Hampton Magna (SMR)*
- 507 – *Cubbington to Leamington Spa (A&M) – Wednesday and Friday*
- 508 – *Leamington to Warwick via Whitnash (A&M)*
- 667 – *Offchurch, Leamington Spa, Warwick (ALC) – school term only*

In addition, some long-distance services pass through this section, such as the National Express 320 from Bradford to Oxford and 460 Stratford to London, both of which pick up in Warwick and Leamington.

Contact details for bus operators in this area are listed below, although Traveline (www.traveline.org.uk) on 0870 6082608 can give details of specific services between 7 a.m. and 10 p.m:

- A&M Group Village Bus (01926 612487)
- A Line Coaches (024 76643200)
- Stagecoach Midland Red (01788 535555)

TAXIS

The following list gives a selection of the taxi operators in this section:

- A1 Taxis, Leamington Spa (01926 335300)
- Aero Taxis, Leamington Spa (01926 314240)
- Ashford Cabs, Whitnash (01926 332481)
- Avon Knight Cars, Leamington Spa (01926 420041)
- Arrows Taxis, Warwick (01926 888855)
- B & R Cars, Warwick (01926 494849)
- Castle Cars of Warwick, Warwick (01926 494989)
- Dial A Cab, Leamington Spa (01926 882965)
- JCB Cabs, Leamington Spa (01926 888866)
- Roman Taxis, Warwick (01926 499996)
- Victoria Cars, Leamington Spa (01926 881161)

SECTION C

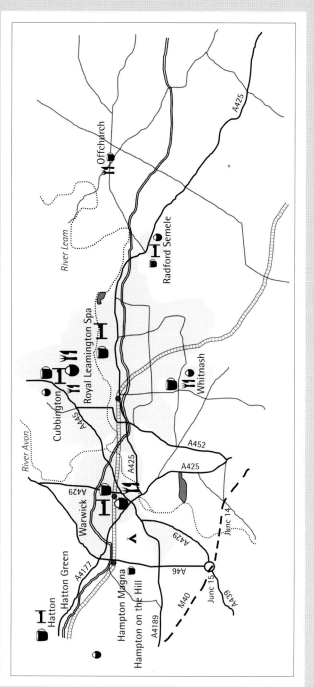

Key

—— Canal
·········· River
▮▮▮▮▮ Railway
– – – Motorway
—— A Road
—— B Road
⬤ Built up area
● Stations
◗ Open water
◖ Shops
🛏 Accomodation
⋀ Campsite
☕ Pub
🍴 Restaurant

BASICS

INTRODUCTION

The two towns of Warwick and Leamington Spa (or, more correctly, Royal Leamington Spa) practically merge into one, but are in fact quite separate areas. These days, Leamington is the more major of the two towns, certainly in terms of shops and supplies, although the centres of each are a brisk walk from the towpath.

Warwick Hospital (01926 495321) just north of the station has an Accident and Emergency Department.

SHOPPING

This section begins with a surprise: Hatton Shopping Village (01926 843411), south of St John's Bridge (No.55) just before the locks, an unlikely spot for a shopping experience. This offers the sorts of goods you can no longer find on the High Street, from clothes to homeware, and a farm shop and shops specialising in things like candles, artificial flowers and stained glass. Also by Hatton is the Hatton Farm Shop (01926 843405) which offers a wide range of cheese as well as the chutneys and bread you need to go with them.

> Developed from a collection of previously redundant Victorian farm buildings, Hatton shopping village also holds regular food and craft fairs during the summer.

While Hatton offers one form of retail therapy, the more mainstream centre for shopping along this stretch is, undoubtedly, Leamington Spa. This is a major regional centre with many of the national High Street names such as House of Fraser and Marks & Spencer, as well as most of the main fashion chains, all featured along the town's main drag, The Parade.

In addition, Leamington has two malls, The Royal Priors and The Regency Arcade. There are also plenty of less high profile, but still interesting, shops on the many side streets off The Parade, along with a number of local shopping parades scattered around the outskirts of the town.

The Old Town should also not be forgotten and includes the area sandwiched between the canal and the Leam, including the railway station, as well as shops further to the south. Leamington also has an out-of-town shopping centre, The Shires, south of Bridge 43, which has a large Sainsbury's. Leamington's Farmer's Market takes place every fourth Saturday of the month in the Pump Room Gardens.

Warwick offers a very different shopping experience from Leamington. What it lacks in recognisable High Street names it more than makes up for in its variety of smaller, often quite specialist shops. Most of these are along a straight run bisected by the magnificent Eastgate building. To the west lies Jury Street and the High Street, the main shopping area, while to the east is Smith Street, which mainly comprises restaurants.

At the bottom of Smith Street there is a run of more secondary shops, including an off-licence and a grocery, and it is this run that leads down to the canal, half a mile away. Like Leamington, Warwick also has a number of local shopping parades with off-licences, pharmacies and the like, and there is a large Tesco right on the canal by Bridge 46. Warwick holds a Farmer's Market on the third Friday of every month in the Market Place.

Porch of St Gregory's church, Offchurch.

To the north of Leamington Spa, Cubbington has a bakery, an old-fashioned hardware/DIY store, a post office and a Costcutter convenience stores in its older heart. There is also a parade of shops in the more recent quarter along the Rugby Road which includes a newsagent, a Mace general stores and some fast-food outlets.

There is a run of shops at Whitnash, including a post office and a One Stop convenience store, as well as a secondary shopping centre in one of the housing estates with a Premier Stores and a tropical fish centre! Radford Semele has a small local shop with an off-licence and ATM.

> The Revd James Austen, brother of the novelist Jane Austen, was the vicar at St Mary's, Cubbington, from 1792 to 1820.

EATING AND DRINKING

Unsurprisingly perhaps, given the long history of the major towns in this section and their position on the road route linking the country's two largest cities, there is no shortage of watering holes within striking distance of the towpath. The following list offers a selection of what is available:

Warwick:
- The Cape of Good Hope, Lower Cape (01926 498138) – *canalside*
- The Crown and Castle, Coten End (01926 492087)
- The Lord Nelson, Emscote Road (01926 494115) – *a short walk up from the canal*
- The Millwright Arms, Coten End (01926 496955)
- The New Bowling Green, St Nicholas Church Street (01926 493642)
- The Oak, Coten End (01926 493774)
- The Racehorse, Stratford Road (01926 496705)
- The Roebuck, Smith Street (01926 494900) – *sixteenth century*
- The Saxon Mill, Coventry Road (01926 492255) – *on the Avon*
- Tudor House Inn, West Street (01926 495447) – *near the castle*
- The Warwick Arms, High Street (01926 492759)

Leamington Spa:

- The Benjamin Satchwell, The Parade (01926 883733)
- The Bowling Green, New Street (07816 907398)
- The Green Man, Tachbrook Street (01926 316298)
- Jug and Jester, Bath Street (01926 425727)
- The Lock, Dock and Barrel, Brunswick St (01926 430333) – *by Bridge 40*
- The Moorings, Myton Road (01926 425043) – *canalside*
- Murphy's, Regent St (01926 832621)
- Newbold Comyn Arms, Newbold Terrace East (01926 338810)
- The Red House, Radford Road (01926 881725)
- Talbot Inn, Rushmore Street (01926 424857)
- The Tiller Pin, Queensway (01926 435139) – *canalside*
- White Horse, Clarendon Avenue (01926 436801)
- Woodland Tavern, Regent Street (01926 425868)
- The Falcon, Hatton (01926 484737)
- The Waterman Inn, Hatton (01926 492427)
- Montgomery of Alamein, Hampton Magna (01926 494266)
- The Kings Head, Cubbington (01926 887142)
- The Queen's Head, Cubbington (01926 429949)
- The Rugby Tavern, Cubbington (01926 423449)
- The Heathcote Inn, Whitnash (01926 428120)
- The Plough and Harrow, Whitnash (01926 428834)
- The Windmill, Whitnash (01926 831214)
- The White Lion, Radford Semele (01926 425770)
- Stags Head, Offchurch (01926 425801)

SECTION C

The main eating quarter in Warwick is clustered around Smith Street, which is so food-orientated that there is even a shop selling 'dining accessories' and another specialising in Far Eastern, North African and Indian cooking utensils. This has the advantage of being the most accessible area from the towpath.

Restaurants in this area include:

- The Cellar Restaurant (01926 400809) – *Mediterranean*
- The Castle Balti, St. Johns (01926 493799) – *just off Smith Street*
- Chopsticks (01926 479188) – *Chinese*
- Giovannist (01926 494904) – *Italian*
- Piccolinos (01926 491020) – *Italian*
- Raj's (01926 400600) – *Indian*
- Robbies (01926 400470) – *vegetarian*

Other restaurants in Warwick include the following, although most of the hotels listed in 'Sleeping' also serve non-residents:

- Charlotte's, Jury Street (01926 498930) – *vegetarian home cooking*
- Fanshawes, Market Place (01926 410590) – *English/French*
- Findons, Old Square (01926 411755) – *modern British*

Well monument, Leamington Spa.

Restaurants in Leamington Spa include the following:

- Casa Valle, Regent Street (01926 741128) – *Italian*
- Chico's, Guy Street (01926 435434) – *Mexican/Texan*
- Emperor's Cantanese, Bath Place (01926 313030) – *Chinese*
- Eleven 11, Regent Place (01926 424723) – *French*
- The Grand Union Restaurant (01926 421323) – *dinner-party style by Bridge 40*
- Jamil, Agusta Place (01926 428620) – *Mediterranean*
- Nicolini's, The Parade (01926 421620) – *Italian*
- Oscars, Chandos Street (01926 452807) – *French*
- Thai Elephant, Regent Street (01926 886882) – *Thai*

Elsewhere the fare is mainly convenience, with one notable exception:

- Blossom Court, Cubbington (01926 334647) – *Chinese takeaway*
- Cubbington Plaice (01926 424381) – *fish and chips*
- Heathcote Fish Bar, Whitnash (01926 435300) – *fish and chips*
- The Prince Regent II, Ham Farm, Offchurch (01608 662216) – *canal boat dining*

There is also a good selection of places to stop and simply take tea or a snack in the picturesque surroundings of Warwick and Leamington and their environs, including the following:

- Hatton Locks Café (01926 409432) – *at the top of the flight*
- Café Déjà Vu, Old Square, Warwick (01926 496840)
- Charlotte's Tea Room, Jury Street, Warwick (01926 498930)
- Continental Café, High Street, Leamington Spa (01926 426841)
- Olive Coffee House, Leamington Spa (01926 888895)
- The Poacher's Den, Warwick (01926 403700) – *tea room*
- Pump Rooms Café/Tea Rooms, Leamington Spa (01926 742751)
- St Nicholas Park Café, Warwick (01926 492962)
- Wylie's Café, The Old Iron Yard, Warwick (01926 402595)

SLEEPING

Thihis section's relative proximity to Stratford, as well as the intrinsic attractions of both Warwick and Leamington Spa, mean this is an area very well provided for with regards to places to stay. The castle in Warwick seems to act as a magnet for smaller hotels and guest houses.

The following is a selection of places to stay in this section:

HOTELS
- Angel Hotel, Leamington Spa (01926 881296) – *47 rooms, town-centre hotel*
- The Aylesford Hotel, Warwick (01926 492799) – *16 rooms, small-town hotel*
- Agincourt Lodge Hotel, Warwick (01926 499399) – *small town-centre hotel*

> The eleven-year-old Princess Victoria stayed at the Regent Hotel in 1830 while travelling to Birmingham, a visit which resulted in Leamington being granted royal status eight years later.

- Cambridge Villa Hotel, Warwick (01926 491169) – *small town-centre hotel*
- Express by Holiday Inn, Warwick 0870 4009068 – *On Junction 15 of the M40*
- Express by Holiday Inn, Warwick (01926 483000) – *town centre*
- Falstaff Hotel, Leamington Spa (01926 312044) – *Best Western*
- Globe Hotel, Warwick (01926 492044) – *Thai-style hotel*
- Hilton Hotel, Warwick (01926 499555) – *out-of-town modern hotel*
- The Lord Leycester Hotel, Warwick (01926 491481) – *prestigious town-centre hotel*
- Marriott Courtyard, Leamington Spa (01926 425522) – *large modern hotel*
- Regent Hotel, Leamington Spa (0870 1911738) – *on the Parade, now a Travelodge*
- Royal Leamington Hotel, Leamington Spa (01926 883777) – *Best Western*
- Tudor House Hotel (01926 495447) – *town-centre inn*
- Victoria Park Hotel, Leamington Spa (01926 424195) – *20 rooms in town centre*
- Warwick Arms Hotel (01926 492759) – *on the High Street*
- The Wheatsheaf Hotel, Warwick (01926 410508) – *sixteenth-century building*

BED AND BREAKFAST/GUEST HOUSES
- The Falcon Inn, Hatton (01926 484737)
- Haseley House Hotel, Hatton (01926 484222) – *old Georgian rectory in own grounds*
- Ashburton Guest House, Warwick (01926 499133)
- Austin House, Warwick (01926 493583)
- The Avon Guest House, Warwick (01926 491367)
- The Coach House, Warwick (01926 410893)
- Chesterfields B&B, Warwick (01926 774864)
- Forth House, Warwick (01926 401512)
- The Park Cottage, Warwick (01926 410319)
- Seven Stars Guest House, Warwick (01926 492658)
- Warwick Lodge, Warwick (01926 492927)

SECTION C

- The Westham Guest House, Warwick (01926 491756)
- Avenue Lodge, Leamington Spa (01926 338555)
- Charnwood Guest House, Leamington Spa (01926 831074)
- Eaton Court, Leamington Spa (01926 885848)
- Garden Café Town House Hotel, Leamington Spa (01926 883561)
- Hedley Villa Guest House, Leamington Spa (01926 424504)
- Trendway Guest House, Leamington Spa (01926 316644)
- Bungalow Farm, Cubbington (01926 423276)
- Bakers Cottage, Cubbington (01926 772146)
- Staddlestones B&B, Cubbington (01926 740253)
- Hill Farm B&B, Radford Semele (01926 337571)

Leamington Spa's Tourist Information Office also runs an Accommodation Service on 01926 742767.

CAMPING

The only camping site along this stretch is at the Warwick Racecourse, a caravan club site that welcomes non-members but is not suitable for tents. The site has fifty-one pitches, although this reduces to thirty-eight on race days so it is worth telephoning ahead.

The nearest camping supplies outlets in this section are:

- Escape 2, Warwick (01926 493929)
- Millets, Leamington Spa (01926 421430)
- Mountain Warehouse, Hatton Country World (01926 842761)
- W Yeomans, Leamington Spa (01926 451276)

Avon Aqueduct, Warwick.

Warwick St Mary's and war memorial.

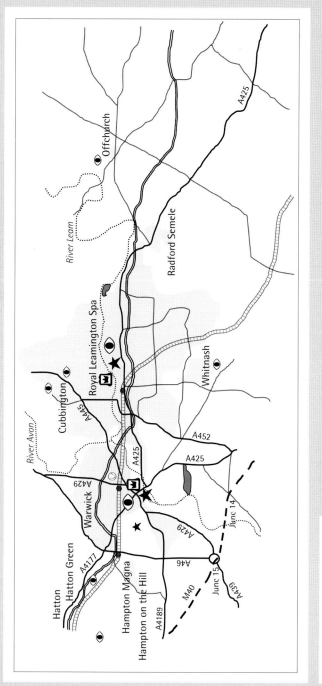

Key

Canal
River
Railway
Motorway
A Road
B Road
Built up area
Stations
Open water
Site/Sight
Leisure
Entertainment
Culture

SEEING AND DOING

INTRODUCTION

Warwick is one of the best examples of an unspoiled historical town in the country and is not always recognised for the gem it is. Those who simply visit its castle will have a good day out but will fail to appreciate the fullness of the town, which is best explored on foot. Likewise, Leamington Spa rewards a stroll; although there is less to see here, it is impossible not to absorb some of the history that oozes out of its walls.

Warwick's Tourist Information Centre is on Jury Street (01926 492212), while Leamington Spa's is in the Royal Pump Rooms (01926 742762).

SIGHTS

Hatton once again begins this section with a bang with the Hatton Farm Village (01926 843411), which is aligned with the Shopping Village to the south. This is dedicated to the discovery of farm animals, offering the opportunity see various animals, experience tractor rides and visit the small funfair.

Also in the vicinity of Hatton is the flight of locks named after the village, occasionally known as the boater's 'Stairway to Heaven'. The locks attract waves of visitors in the summer, both boaters wrestling with the twenty-one locks involved and gongoozlers happy to watch them. The towpath here is firm and easy, although it is uphill! BW's old workshops are also an attraction, not least for the colourful restored boats that often moor here.

> Damselflies, with blue tails and bands, hover around the locks in the summer. After spending five years in the water as larva, their stay lasts for just weeks – enough time to mate and lay eggs.

While Leamington may be the more prominent shopping focus in this section, the honours go to Warwick when it comes to things to see. The jewel in the town's crown is its castle (0870 442 2000), which sells itself as Britain's 'Greatest Medieval Experience'. It is easy to spend a day here enjoying the mix of sheer grandeur, pleasant gardens and grounds, undeniable history and at times unashamed tourist additions (such as waxworks), and it would be a shame to come to Warwick and miss it.

There is more to Warwick than its castle though, and the towpath traveller is advised to get one of the trails available from the Tourist Information Centre and pick their own way around the town's compact but history-filled centre. The most obvious sight is the Lord Leycester Hospital (01926 491422), originally an old soldier's home and later home to Warwick's Guilds; today this is an impressive set of timber-framed buildings clustered around a Norman Gateway.

Other sights that might be missed include the Collegiate Church of St Mary on Old Square (01926 403940), with its Medieval and Tudor tombs and impressive roof, Oken's House and Doll Museum (01926 495546) on Castle Street, and

> The Tink-a-Tank, which leads round the churchyard to the Butts, was given this name from the sound of boots echoing between the stone walls either side. Look out for the College Garden off a gate in the lane.

Mill Street, where it is possible to see a row of houses that survived the great fire of 1694.

The Eastgate and Landor House, both at the junction of Jury Street and Smith Street, are also both worth seeing. The former was once a chapel but today is part of a girl's school, while the latter, also part of the same school, was once the Maidenhead Inn and was later the birthplace of the poet Walter Savage Landor.

Another highlight is the former County Gaol near the Shire Hall. This was rebuilt after the fire but retained its bottle-shaped dungeon; a ventilator from the dungeon can be seen in the courtyard. The hall itself was saved from the fire and is still used by the Crown Court, and has a hall and two octagonal courts.

These are only some of the buildings that can be seen during a casual stroll through Warwick. More formal attractions include the Warwickshire Museum (01926 412500), which contains the Warwickshire Bear, and St John's Museum (01926 412132), a Jacobean mansion with a reconstructed Victorian parlour, kitchen and classroom.

The latter also houses the Royal Warwickshire Regimental Museum (01926 491653), which shows the history of the 'Warwickshire Lads'. It houses a collection of objects connected to the Regiment, where it is also possible to don a soldier's uniform and hear veterans' experiences of D-Day

> The (stuffed) Warwickshire Bear used to grace Wroxhall Abbey where it stood in the hallway with a silver platter to accept visitors' calling cards. One theory claimed it was shot in Alaska, while another suggests it came from a travelling circus and died of natural causes.

and Gallipoli. This is one of three militia-related museums, the others being the Warwickshire Yeomanry Museum (01926 492212) and the Queen's Own Hussar's Museum (01926 492035), which is within the Lord Leycester Hospital.

One of the main attractions in Leamington is the Royal Pump Rooms (01926 742762), which was recently redeveloped into an art gallery and museum, and also houses the Tourist Information Centre and a café. The museum is the place to head if you are keen to learn more about the town's spa side, and includes a Turkish Room and history on Victorian spa activities.

For a quieter time, head for the Hill Close Victorian Gardens (01926 493216) between the old town walls and the racecourse, an oasis of calm which was saved by local residents as an example of a Victorian detached garden, and which has no less than nine summer houses. Another similar oasis is the Master's Garden within the Lord Leycester Hospital.

Leamington is known for its open spaces and The Pump Rooms sit within the Royal Pump Room Gardens, once the exclusive preserve of visitors taking the waters, which sits over the road from the comprehensive Jephson Gardens. The gardens have a bandstand as well as a number of other attractions such as fountains, a clock tower and an obelisk, as well as a Riverside Walk.

Also in Leamington are Landsdowne Crescent and Landsdowne Circus, impressive regency buildings designed by William Thomas. The author Nathaniel Hawthorne stayed at No.10, a bolthole he called his 'little nest'. The parish church of All Saints by the river is a good example of Gothic Revival and is one of the largest parish churches in the country, extended in stages between 1843 and 1902.

Heritage boats **Scorpio** *and* **Malus** *at Hatton.*

Look out for the monument over the road which was erected in 2000 to mark the spot where the first well tapping the town's spring was located, and for the ramp down to the river, constructed to allow resident circus elephants to take the water. Those with the stomach, in all senses of the word, can still sample the water in the Pump Rooms.

Cubbington Brewery (01926 450747), home of the Warwickshire Beer Co., stands out on Queen Street in Cubbington. Founded in 1998 on the site of an old bakery, the brewery produces two bottled and seven cask beers, and will offer tours by appointment.

Parts of St Mary's Church at Cubbington date back to the twelfth century and the present building has an impressive timber roof with tie beams running from wall to wall resting on main rafters. The stone font dates back to the twelfth or thirteenth century, while the more modern Te Deum window in the Chancel was dedicated in 1902.

St Margaret's church at Whitnash was extended by the Victorian architect Sir Gilbert Scott, and has a fine collection of stained glass and ancient brasses, and before leaving this area it is also worth visiting the church at Offchurch, St Gregorys. Enter via the impressive porch and on a sunny day you will immediately be bathed in blue light from the Millennium Window, designed by local stained-glass expert, Roger Sargeant. The church has three Saxon windows in the chancel and a priest's door in the side.

CULTURE AND ENTERTAINMENT

Both Warwick and Leamington Spa are well endowed with cultural attractions. When it comes to theatre, Warwick has The Dream Factory (01926 419555), home of the Playbox Theatre Co. which focuses on drama involving young people, while Leamington has the Loft Theatre (01926 426341).

For more static art there is the Warwick Gallery in Smith Street, which specialises in the work of British artists, as well as The Gallery, in Swan Street (01926 495506). Leamington has its own gallery at the Pump Rooms (01926 742700).

The area is also lucky to have two major arts venues, the Warwick Arts Centre (024 7652 4524) at Warwick University, slightly out of town, and the Royal Spa Centre (01926 334418) in Leamington. The former is a major regional centre and hosts theatre, cinema, dance, comedy and concerts, as well as being home to the Mead Gallery which exhibits art and photography.

> Warwick University is named after the county rather than the town, and is in fact nearer to Coventry.

The Royal Spa Centre has an 800-seat theatre and a cinema with its own Spa Theatre Co. Shows vary from ballet to wrestling, and include musical performances ranging from jazz to the classics. Leamington also has the Apollo Cinema (0871 223 3449) showing mainstream films.

For more active pursuits, Warwick has the St Nicholas Park Leisure Centre (01926 495353) which has a six-lane swimming pool with splash pool, as well as gym and sports hall, while Leamington has the Newbold Comyn Leisure Centre

> The first tennis club in the world was formed at Leamington in 1872, behind the Manor House Hotel, and the modern rules of lawn tennis were drawn up here two years later.

(01926 882083) which has a pool with flume and poolside sauna as well as a gym and aerobics studio. There is also ten-pin bowling at the Megaplex in Shires Retail Park (01926 885444).

For younger folk there is also Funky Monkeys soft play (01926 409007), which lies to the north of the town but is convenient for the towpath. Other recreation for children can be found at the St Nicholas Gardens where there is an adventure playground, swimming/paddling pool, adventure golf and a skateboard park – as well as riverside walks and a picnic area.

Warwick Racecourse (01926 491553) is a national standard racecourse featuring flat and jump racing all year round, as well as children's entertainment on race days.

When it comes to nightlife, Leamington offers the most choice, with the following a selection of available clubs:

- Club Mirage, Leamington Spa
  (01926 435310)
- Club Silk, Leamington Spa
  (01926 311755)
- Options, Leamington Spa
  (01926 311755)
- Rios, Leamington Spa
  (01926 421383)
- Sugar, Leamington Spa
  (01926 422223)

In addition, Radford Semele Sports and Social Club (01926 330314) features regular live bands.

> Leamington is home to the modern folk band Nizlopi, who had the Christmas 2005 Number One single with their song *JCB*.

Part of Jephson Gardens, Leamington.

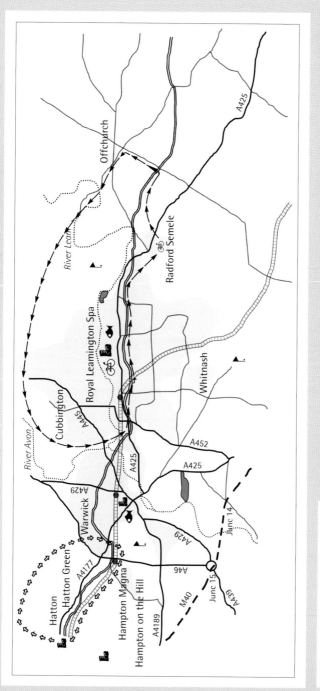

Key

— Canal
······ River
╫╫╫╫ Railway
– – – Motorway
—— A Road
—— B Road
▨ Built up area
◗ Stations
◗ Open water
🚲➝ Cycling route/ outlet
👢➝ Walking route/ outlet
🐟 Fishing spot/ outlet
⌐ Golf course/ outlet
Ω Riding outlet

SAMPLING

INTRODUCTION

A reasonable network of paths means it is relatively easy to sample this section, with the canal providing a convenient link between Warwick and Leamington. The two rivers offer variety and there are plenty of places to leave the car and explore the wider countryside. The section is mostly covered by OS Explorer Map 221, Coventry and Warwick, just spilling over into Explorer 222, Rugby and Daventry.

WALKING

This section sits in the middle of the Centenary Way, a 98 (not, for some reason, 100) mile route created to celebrate the centenary of Warwickshire County Council. The route passes through the north of Warwick, to the east of the Wedgnock Rifle Range and joins the towpath at Bridge 49, leaving it for a while to take in the River Leam before rejoining the canal at Bridge 37 and heading east until Bridge 31, before heading south.

Alternatively, the Offchurch Greenway is a flat and surfaced walking and cycling route, 1.5 miles long, which forms part of Sustrans Route 41. Originally part of the Leamington to Rugby railway line, the route can be accessed from a small (free) car park at the mid-point of Offchurch Cross Roads.

The area to the east of Leamington Spa, taking in the Newbold Comyn Park, is also a popular walking spot with a number of footpaths, some of which head north into Cubbington. Similarly, parts of the River Leam can be followed west of Offchurch.

If your bent is more urban, do not forget the Town Trail available from the Warwick Tourist Information Office, the various parks in Leamington Spa or the well-signposted Riverside Walk between Warwick and Leamington. Nature reserves in this section include Whitnash Brook between Whitnash and Radford Semele, and the Oakwood and Blacklow Spinney just north of Bridge 49.

Walk C takes in the main towpath feature of this walk, the Hatton Flight, as well as the chance to appreciate the well-tended gardens along the Saltisford Arm.

The well-maintained Saltisford Arm just outside Warwick.

SECTION C WALK
Hatton Flight and back via Hatton and Saltisford

Description:	*A relatively easy walk, although the flight naturally includes an incline!*
Distance:	*5.5 miles*
Duration:	*2.5 hours*
Starting point:	*Grid Reference 243669, OS Explorer 221 Coventry and Warwick*
Nearest refreshment:	*The Waterman, Hatton*

Start from the parking at Bridge 54 at the top of the flight. Head north with the white house on your right and pass through a kissing gate and past the Waterman, turning right beside it. Follow the road to the fork on the left where you bear left and then left again up a minor road by a stream.

Follow the bridleway on your right after around a quarter of a mile and follow this to Turkey Farm, passing the old Hatton Sanatorium on the way. Pass through a metal gate alongside a farmhouse and skirt a pond. On reaching a marker, walk around the edge of a field and go through a gap on the left near an oak tree, following this path to the far corner and turning right. Continue with the Blackbrake Plantation on your left and keep with the path as it zigzags to Wedgnock Park Farm.

Follow the track to the right of the farm all the way down to the road. Cross by the traffic lights and take Budbrook Road ahead and over the canal bridge, turning left at the footpath by the cemetery. Head off left and through a gap onto the towpath, where you turn right. To your left is the Saltisford Arm and there is a chance to divert to take this in. Otherwise, follow the flight uphill back to your starting point.

Walking equipment outlets along this section include:

- Escape 2, Warwick (01926 493929)
- Millets, Leamington Spa (01926 889012)
- Mountain Warehouse, Hatton Country World (01926 842761)
- Yeomans, Leamington Spa (01926 451276)

CYCLING

The relative paucity of minor roads along this section mean that cyclists have to be careful when constructing routes. That said, the towpath and other routes mentioned above make for plenty of alternatives.

A suggested route for sampling this section by bike starts in Radford Semele and heads down to Bull Bridge (No.34) by the White Lion. Turn right onto the towpath and past the first of the two Fosse Locks, turning left at Bridge 32 and north to Springhill Cottages on the Fosse Way. Turn left here and into

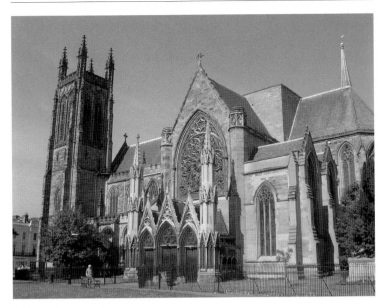

All Saints church, Leamington Spa.

Offchurch over the old railway. Stick with the Welsh Road all the way into Cubbington, taking the first fork left.

Cross over the Rugby Road and the A445, and on reaching White Gates head left, over the A452 and along the Old Milverton Road, which becomes Sandy Lane, sticking with this as it heads south just before Church Farm. Follow this to the A445 where you turn right and then almost immediately left and then right again before the railway line. Follow this road as it crosses the Leam and reaches a roundabout. Here you pick up the towpath, heading right at Bridge 42, sticking with it to Bridge 35 where you turn right and back into Radford Semele, a total of around 13 miles.

Cycle outlets along this section include:

- Broadribbs, Leamington Spa (01926 421428)
- Kelvin Cycles, Leamington Spa (01926 423308)
- John Atkins Cycles, Leamington Spa (01926 883122)
- Smiths Cycles, Leamington Spa (01926 425742)

RIDING

The Bridleway used in Walk C is one of the most prominent tracks in this section. This heads north by Turkey Farm and skirts the Larch Covert danger area before joining Centenary Way. Alternatively, there is a track heading south-east before reaching the danger area which takes you back to the Cape area of western Warwick.

Horse-riding establishments and outlets along this section include:

- Horsecare, Hatton (01926 484483)
  – *stables with grazing and a sand
  ménage, access to good hacking*

- The Warwick International School
  of Riding, Warwick (01926 494313)
  – *includes cross-country course and
  1-mile sand gallops.*

FISHING

Those wishing to fish the canal along this section are advised to consult one of the two local outlets listed below as it is not always clear under whose jurisdiction the waters belong. The Rover Gaydon Angling Club (01203 462767) is listed as controlling the waters around the Hatton Flight, while the Warwick and District Angling Society (01455 220045) is also active.

The Rivers Leam and Avon seem to be preferred by local anglers, with the Warwick and District AS organising an annual Saxon Mill Angling Festival on the Avon north of the canal. This also involves water run by the Leamington Spa and Farringtons Angling Clubs.

The first of these controls most of the fishing on the Leam from Offchurch, through Leamington and on to the junction with the Avon. Chub are a good catch here with roach and bream also plentiful around the weir pool at Princes Drive.

Outlets selling fishing supplies along this stretch include:

- Baileys Fishing Tackle, Warwick (01926 491984)
- Old Town Tackle, Leamington Spa (01926 421855)

OTHER

Adventure Sports (01926 491948) at the Wedgnock Rifle Range north of Warwick provide a different way of sampling the area with tanks and amphibious vehicles to drive, paintballing, off-road courses and clay-pigeon shooting.

Otherwise, there is a good selection of golf courses along the section, including:

- Leamington and County Golf Club,
  Whitnash (01926 425961) –
  18 holes, 6,439 yards
- Newbold Comyn Golf Course,
  Leamington Spa (01926 421157)
  *– 18 holes municipal course with
  9-hole pitch and putt, 6,315 yards*

- Warwick Racecourse Golf Club
  (01926 494316) – *9 holes, 2,682
  yards*
- The Warwickshire Golf Club (01926
  409409) – *36 Championship holes
  and a 9-hole, par-3 course, 7,154
  and 7,178 yards*

SECTION D

LONG ITCHINGTON TO NORTON JUNCTION

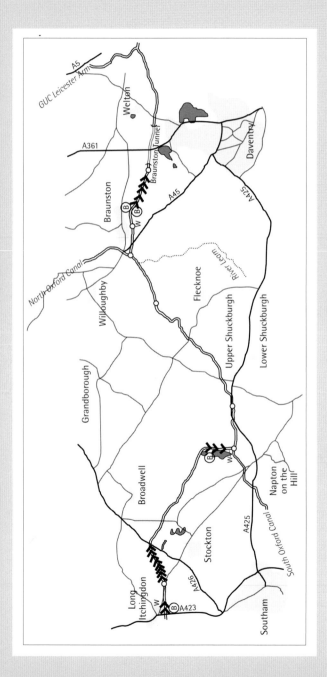

SHAPERS

THE CANAL ON THIS STRETCH

KEY FACTS

LENGTH: 13.25 miles

BOATYARDS: 3
> Warwickshire Fly Boat Co.
> Blue Lias Marina
> Calcutt Boats

WATERPOINTS: 3
> Stockton Top Lock
> Calcutt Bottom Lock
> Braunston Stop House

TURNING POINTS: 7
> Stockton Top Lock
> Napton Junction
> Bridge 107
> Wolfhampcote
> Braunston Turn
> Braunston Stop House
> Braunston Tunnel West Portal

LOCKS: 19
> Itchington Bottom Lock (6ft 7in)
> Calcutt Locks (16ft 2in)
> Stockton Locks (9) (54ft 7in)
> Braunston Flight (6) (35ft 6in)

This section is largely independent of the nearby villages and as such the towpath is relatively unused, so it is often bumpy and difficult to move along. This is particularly the case between Napton and Braunston, with the towpath beside the locks either side of these two providing some respite.

Soon after leaving Long Itchington two locks presage the Stockton flight, a total of eight closely packed together on a straight section of canal, with the short Kaye's Arm running off to the right before the flight begins. Also here is the base of the Warwickshire Fly Boat Co., which has a small shop selling chandlery and ice cream, and the Blue Lias pub. Mooring here is long-term only.

The Stockton Top Marina, with more long-term towpath moorings, marks the end of the flight, after which the canal makes a sweep to the right. The towpath loses its previously firm nature and the bankside is quite overgrown

Stockton Locks.

in places along this section. The water executes a gentle curve to the right after Bridge 20 and another to the right after the following bridge where the canal widens momentarily.

A long, straight section follows, with the large Ventnor Farm marina on the left. The towpath regains its previous solid nature in the run up to the three Calcutt Locks which appear after a bend to the right. Water can be taken on at the end of the locks, where there is also the Calcutt Boats yard, which has a small shop selling basics. The towpath reverts to turf and starts its long, straight run into Napton Junction, with a new marina straight in front.

Turn left at the junction where there is a short straight, a prelude to a decidedly wobbly part of the canal, with the towpath becoming less even in sympathy. The A425 crosses over at Bridge 108 and again at the next bridge, before passing to the left of Lower Shuckburgh. The course from here is relatively straight but uninspiring for a while, with the towpath becoming really quite narrow and very bumpy in places.

The canal swings to the left after Bridge 103 and then wildly to the right after the following bridge, before resuming its previous direction. Another 180-degree manoeuvre follows, after which there is a straight, alongside which the towpath finally firms up a bit. A curve to the right follows after Bridge 99, where the bank becomes reinforced and suitable for mooring, with the opposite bank here colonised by more permanent craft.

It is possible to wind along here and after a temporary aberration the towpath regains its previous state. Soon the dominant spire of All Saints church in Braunston appears and the twin iron bridges of Braunston Turn follow. Cross over these turning right, after which there is a long run of moorings leading up to the Stop House and beyond, all the way to the forthcoming locks, some of which are long-stay.

The towpath passes the Millhouse pub on the opposite bank (accessible from Bridge 91) as well as a couple of water points (one outside the Stop House).

An arched iron bridge takes you over the entrance to Braunston Marina. Understandably, this is a popular spot and boaters need to grab whatever moorings they can get during busy parts of the year.

> Braunston Tunnel is 2,042 yards long and 16ft wide, and lined with three layers of bricks. A distinct kink in the centre betrays the fact that it was cut from each end and failed to meet.

A stepped wooden bridge takes you over the back entrance/exit to the marina and onto Braunston Boats, a busy working boatyard, as well as the base for Union Canal Carriers. Just by here you can also see the old Pump House which used to house a Boulton & Watt engine used to pump water back to the top of the locks.

The first of six locks now follows, with the useful Boat Shop (01788 891310) soon after. This has a comprehensive selection of canal-related books as well as home-baked bread and other basic provisions. A short, straight section just before the tunnel incorporates the last three locks, with the entrance to the tunnel itself the usual modest affair with a short winding hole just before it.

It is possible to walk over the top of the tunnel using a footpath which follows an old track. This takes you over the top of the hill and past a couple of air shafts. The canal remerges in woods and follows a straight before kinking left and leading up to Norton Junction, where the solid towpath before the canal gives way to bumpier ground.

PRINCIPAL TOWNS AND VILLAGES ALONG THIS STRETCH

BRAUNSTON:
The tower of All Saints church and the adjacent windmill at one end of Braunston's main street provide twin beacons which can be seen for miles around. The village itself is set off from the canal on a hill but is easily accessible and well worth a visit.

BROADWELL:
Apart from its large green, Broadwell's most distinguishing feature is probably its tiny village hall which is made out of green corrugated iron. There is a Millennium Stone nearby.

> For many years the BBC World Service was broadcast from a large antenna based just outside Daventry, and the station was also used to give the first demonstration of radar in 1935.

DAVENTRY:
Daventry's wide High Street betrays the town's past as a coaching stop and market centre, although recent growth means the outskirts are more modern.

FLECKNOE:
A very desirable village with spectacular views which exploit its hilltop position.

GRANDBOROUGH:
The tall spire of St Peter's church, along with the local pub, are the two main features of this attractive village tucked away from all the surrounding main roads.

LONG ITCHINGTON:

Although sitting on the A423, Long Itchingdon is worth a pause for its pond, its older heart and its position on the side of the canal, something exploited by no less than two pubs, the first of many in this village.

LOWER SHUCKBURGH:

Although accessible from the canal via Bridge 104, Lower Shuckburgh is mainly a collection of farm buildings and, although attractive, has little to interest the causal visitor beyond its Victorian church with its unusual octagonal tower.

NAPTON ON THE HILL:

The name Napton translates from the Celtic to mean 'the farm in the knap of the hill', and the hill upon which Napton stands is its defining feature, along with the windmill which sits on top of it.

SOUTHAM:

A small market town with a compact centre and a sprawl of modern housing on its outskirts, Southam offers a surprising mix of historical buildings and connections. It has had its own town market since Henry III granted it a charter in 1227, and was for a time owned by the Priors of Coventry.

> Southam is mentioned in Shakespeare's *Henry VI Part 3* as the place where Warwick the Kingmaker's ally, Clarence, had gathered his forces.

STOCKTON:

Cocooned at the bottom of a hill, Stockton has seen significant growth in recent years and now sustains a school, a church and two pubs.

UPPER SHUCKBURGH:

Upper Shuckburgh basically comprises Shuckburgh Hall and Park, where it is possible to see herds of deer roaming the foot of the Shuckburgh Hills.

WELTON:

With its church and older core both on top of a hill, Welton is a village of mixed architectural styles positioned to the east of the A361.

WILLOUGHBY:

A small village tucked away to the west of the A45 that retains its Manor House and moat.

SECTION D

HISTORY

This section includes many villages and small towns that have shown a remarkable resilience to the steady march of history. The predominant theme is of small rural villages going their own way, driven more by the seasonal cycle than outside events, with only Southam and Daventry really having their destinies driven by events largely beyond their control.

Most of the smaller villages can trace their origins back to Saxon times; Braunston, for example, is named after the Saxon Brant or Brand and features in a royal charter of 956AD when King Eadwig passed this part of his land to

Fawsley, one of his retinue. Flecknoe's name is also Saxon in origin – meaning 'Flecca's hill-spur' – as is Napton's.

Broadwell, Grandborough and Napton were significant enough to feature in the Domesday Book, but like many of the settlements along this section they were unremarkable, the small populations who lived there earning their living from the soil. Much later on some of these villages grew on the back of local industries, such as Stockton and Broadwell, both of which supplied men to the local cement works. Later, the canal also had an impact on some villages, most notably on Braunston which sat at the junction with the Oxford Canal, although in most cases the canal managed to avoid actually passing through the heart of any of them.

> The fossil of a large Ichthysosaurus was unearthed at Stockton in 1898, and is now in the Natural History Museum.

Napton made a brief bid for local prominence when it was granted a market charter by Edward II but, although the market was significant for a while, it died out over time. Meanwhile, Daventry evolved into the local market town serving the east of the area during the thirteenth century and in 1576 was made a borough by Elizabeth I.

By the time of the Civil War, Daventry was of sufficient size to host Charles I and his troops on the eve of the Battle of Naseby in 1645, but managed to remain relatively unscathed by larger national events. Southam, too, felt the effects of these events and was the location of one of the first skirmishes of the war, although it made its mark the year before when the king passed through the town and the churchwardens refused to ring the bells to make him welcome.

Furious with this behaviour, the king had the church doors locked until they agreed to pay a fine of 13s 4d. The story did not end there, however, as the bell ringers continued their defiance by refusing to ring the bells to wish him 'Godspeed' as he left, leading the king to levy a further 5s fine.

SECTION D

At the top of Calcutt Locks.

Southam's skirmish came about when Parliamentary forces led by Lord Brooke heard that a cavalier force led by the Earl of Nottingham was approaching. Brooke ordered an attack which resulted in a handful of deaths. Southam's position meant it became a favourite spot for gathering armies. King Charles himself slept at the Manor House on Market Hill and Cromwell was also a visitor, along with 7,000 troops, in 1645.

In the same way that the coming of the canal failed to really transform the area, the impact of the railways was minimal. Lines were built – a long stretch of disused track still exists which broadly follows the line of the canal – but these tended to be branch lines, although Braunston and Willoughby shared a station on the former Great Central Line. If anything, the railways had a detrimental effect on the stagecoach trade, with the building of the London to Birmingham railway in 1838 having a particularly disastrous effect. Daventry itself was not connected to the main line until 1888.

Small industries in Daventry, such as shoe making, continued to serve the local economy, although the town received a boost in the 1950s when a large ball-bearing manufacturer set up in the town. In more recent times the town has grown as a distribution centre and as an overspill destination from Birmingham, while many of the smaller centres have survived by becoming attractive for commuters and retired people and, as such, have developed as modern communities.

THE NATURAL LANDSCAPE

The west of this section sits in the broad flat Leam Valley, rising to the south along the ironstone hills that form the Northants/Warwickshire border. A characteristic of this area is Blue Lias clay, which in the past led to the growth of a number of cement works and disused quarries, many of which are now full of water. Blue Lias is also significant for being rich in fossils.

The hills of Napton and Shuckburgh to the south are particularly distinctive, while the route through Braunston follows a gap. Daventry to the south-east of the section is home to the two main sources of ground water in the two reservoirs to its north, although Napton also has a large reservoir, as does Stockton, although this is much smaller. Woodland is thin on the ground, the landscape being dominated by large open fields for most of the way, the exception being Shuckburgh.

ACCESS AND TRANSPORT

ROADS

The A425 linking Southam with Daventry is the main road through this section, providing an east–west thoroughfare. The A423 passes to the north from Southam and links up with Long Itchington, while the A426 strikes out north-east before the road gets there.

Daventry itself is something of a nodal point, with the A45 heading out north-west and through Braunston on its way to Rugby, while the A361 heads due north to link up with the A5, which makes only a brief appearance to the east of the section, beyond which lies the M1. Otherwise, villages tend to be linked with a network of often very minor roads.

RAIL

This used to be an area rich in railway stations, but Beeching's knife was particularly sharp in this section and today there are no live lines at all. The nearest station to Daventry is Long Buckby to the north-east, otherwise Leamington Spa serves the population to the west (see Sections B and C). National Train Enquiries can be reached on 08457 484950.

BUSES

The following list sets out the main bus services servicing this section although it is advisable to check before using them as some buses only run on certain days and others may have been withdrawn since publication of this Guide. It is also worth checking for more local services:

- GA01 – *Banbury to Rugby via Daventry, Braunston and Willoughby (Amos)*
- GA04 – *Daventry to Birmingham via Braunston and Willoughby (Amos)*
- 1/2 – *Southam Circular via Napton and Lower Shuckburgh (Johnsons)*
- 63/64 – *Leamington Spa to Stockton via Southam (SMR)*
- 214 – *Napton, Shuckburgh, Flecknoe (A&M)*
- 500 – *Southam to Long Itchington via Napton (A&M)*
- 503 – *Long Itchington to Southam via Napton and Southam (CC)*

Contact details for bus operators in this area are listed below, although Traveline (www.traveline.org.uk) on 0870 6082608 can give details of specific services between 7 a.m. and 10 p.m.:

- A&M Group Village Bus (01926 612487)
- Amos (01327 260522)
- Cattralls Coaches (01926 813840)
- Johnsons (01564 797000)
- Stagecoach Midland Red (01788 535555)

TAXIS

The following list gives a selection of the taxi operators in this section:

- Cardall's Century, Southam (01926 812145)
- Carol's Cabs, Daventry (01327 876900)
- Curtis Cars, Southam (01926 811517)
- Executive Cars, Southam (01926 817878)
- Marshalls Cars, Long Itchington (01926 812711)
- Silver Cab Company, Daventry (01327 700011)
- T Taxis, Daventry (01327 300666)
- Tony's Taxi, Daventry (01327 311311)

SECTION D

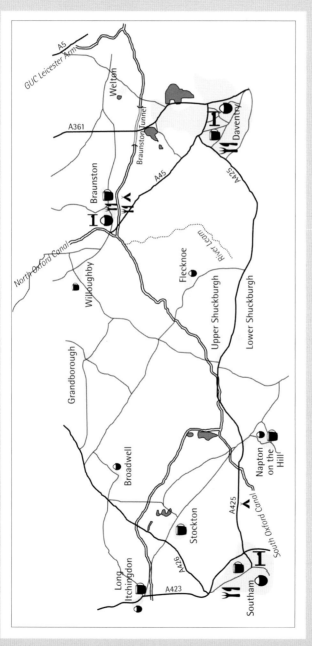

A5
GUC Leicester Arm
Welton
A361
Braunston Tunnel
Daventry
Braunston
A45
A425
North Oxford Canal
Willoughby
Flecknoe
River Leam
Upper Shuckburgh
Lower Shuckburgh
Grandborough
Broadwell
Napton on the Hill
Stockton
South Oxford Canal
A425
Long Itchingdon
A426
A423
Southam

Key
━━━ Canal
············· River
▥▥▥▥ Railway
― ― ― Motorway
──── A Road
──── B Road
● Built up area
● Stations
◗ Open water
🛍 Shops
I Accomodation
⋏ Campsite
🍺 Pub
🍴 Restaurant

BASICS

INTRODUCTION

While pleasant enough to pass through, this section suffers from a sense of being neither one thing nor the other in towpath terms, acting more as a link with other canals (the North Oxford, the South Oxford, the Leicester Arm) and as such almost suffers from an identity crisis.

This is reflected in its lack of focus. Although both Southam and Daventry form part of the section, neither are 'of' the canal. Only Braunston has any real claim to being a canal village (although Long Itchington may beg to differ), and even here the main village is stuck some distance away up a hill.

SHOPPING

The towpath runs to the south of Long Itchington and although there are some shops here they are a short stroll away in the hidden heart of the village. Here there is a newsagent and a Co-op Late Shop with an ATM and post office.

Further south, more than a walk away from the canal, lies Southam, whose High Street also has a Co-op Late Store and an Acorn Stores convenience store as well as a post office and a pharmacy. There is also a selection of more specialist stores as well as a range of banks. Further down Market Hill on Oxford Street in Southam there is a Budgens supermarket.

The store in Napton, again a stroll away from the towpath and more easily accessed from the South Oxford Canal, sells food and offers a wide range of services including an ATM, off-licence and an in-store bakery. Basic chandlery and boat supplies are also available at the marina.

The outlying villages offer some basic supplies, with Broadwell having a farm shop and Flecknoe a bespoke butchers (The Chopping Block 01788 890228), but are generally are too small to support a local store.

If your transport options are limited, Braunston undoubtedly offers the best opportunity to stock up on basic supplies. The village can look inaccessible but is easily reached via Butcher's Bridge (No.1). Here there is a bona fide Village Stores complete with post office as well as a family butcher and a tea shop selling secondhand books and CDs, useful if your stocks of entertainment are running low.

Perhaps more promising on the books front is the Boat Shop by the bottom lock, which carries one of the most comprehensive stocks of canal-related books in the country, as well as provisions and souvenirs. The Marina also has a good stock of books and chandlery.

Although on paper Daventry looks promising in terms of its size, on closer inspection it is disappointing, and has been awaiting a major redevelopment for some time now. There is a town-centre Somerfield which links with a more traditional High Street via Boundary Walk. Here you will find a Waitrose and shops selling most other basic supplies. The town also hosts a Farmer's Market on the first Saturday of the month and has an impressive Market Cross at the end of the High Street.

SECTION D

Finally, outside of town, Halls Barn Farm (01327 702014) sells organic potatoes from the farm gate in season, and also has organic beef and lamb in packs.

EATING AND DRINKING

While the villages along this section may be unable to support a shop, most have, thankfully, been able to retain their 'local', and there are a number of fine drinking holes along this stretch to explore. Some have been successfully converted into fine dining establishments, while others have retained more of a traditional pub feel, and part of the fun of exploring this section is the serendipity on offer.

A selection of the pubs along this section includes:

- The Blue Lias, Long Itchington (01926 812249) – *by Bridge 23*
- The Buck and Bell, Long Itchington (01926 811177)
- The Cuttle, Long Itchington (01926 812314) – *own visitors' moorings*
- The Duck on the Pond, Long Itchington (01926 815876) – *Gastro Pub of the Year, 2004*
- The Green Man, Long Itchington (01926 812208)
- The Harvester, Long Itchington (01926 812698) – *cosy real ale pub*
- The Two Boats, Long Itchington (01926 812640) – *live music on Saturday nights*
- The Black Dog, Southam (01926 813175)
- The Bowling Green, Southam (01926 812575)
- The Bull Inn, Southam (01926 812505)
- The Crown Inn, Southam (01926 810622)
- The Olde Mint, Southam (01926 812339)
- The Barley Mow, Stockton (01926 812713)
- The Crown Inn, Stockton (01926 812255)
- The Crown, Napton (01926 812484)
- The Folly, Napton (01926 815185)
- The Kings Head, Napton (01926 812202)
- The Shoulder of Mutton, Grandborough (01788 810306)

> The Rose at Willoughby was originally called the Four Crosses, and before that, the Three Crosses. Legend has it that the name changed when the author Jonathan Swift had an argument with the landlord's wife and engraved on a window pane: 'You have three crosses on the door, hang up your wife and she'll make four'.

- The Rose Inn, Willoughby (01788 891464)
- The Old Olive Bush, Flecknoe (01788 890318)

> A small building next to the Admiral Nelson in Braunston was originally used for storing salt, as well as the bodies of dead boaters awaiting burial.

- The Admiral Nelson, Braunston (01788 890075)
- The Millhouse, Braunston (01788 890450) – *family pub and dining on the A45 and canal with limited moorings*
- The Old Plough, Braunston (01788 890000)

> The Crown Inn in Stockton is also the HQ of the Half Crown Pétanque Club, which entered the Guinness Book of Records in 1999 after a twenty-four-hour pétanque marathon.

- The Wheatsheaf, Braunston
  (01788 890748) – *does Chinese
  takeaways*
- The George, Daventry
  (01327 702555)
- The Pike and Eel, Daventry
  (01327 703103)

- The Plume of Feathers, Daventry
  (01327 702378)
- The Saracen's Head, Daventry
  (01327 314800)
- The White Horse, Welton
  (01327 702820)
- Zoo, Daventry
  (01327 702027)

Other than the pubs, the towpath traveller's best bet for snacks and lunches along this section are either the marinas or Braunston, where there is the Gongoozler's Rest outside the Stop House as well as the coffee shop in the village and a fish and chip shop, The Braunston Fryer (01788 890258). Further afield, Southam also offers fish and chips at the Seastar (01926 814458), as well as the Courtyard Café (01926 815134) and Efes Takeaway (01926 812568), both of which are on the High Street.

Daventry also has its fair share of 'chippys', including The Danetre (01327 702591) and Michael's Golden Chippy (01327 703807), as well as a selection of tea shops, including:

- Bev's Café (01327 310201)
- Bishop's Tea Rooms (01327 872687)
- The Milk Bar, Daventry
  (01327 702864)

- Upper Crust Coffee Shop
  (01327 702222)

For more substantial fare away from the pubs and hotels, once again Southam and Daventry are the best places to head, although the Wheatsheaf in Braunston (01788 891997) also incorporates the Eastern Chef, offering Chinese and Thai takeaways.

The Blue Lias pub by Bridge 23.

Broadwell's village hall.

Asian food is also the predominant theme in both Southam and Daventry, with one or two exceptions where you can try one of the following:

- Balti Hut, Southam (01926 815948) – *Indian*
- Brook Street Bistro, Daventry (01327 301104)
- China Hall, Southam (01926 812256) – *Chinese*
- Hollywood Nites Diner, Daventry (01327 876600) – *American*
- Mumbai Blues, Southam (01926 817847) – *Indian*
- New India Cottage, Daventry (01327 301924) – *Indian*
- Papadums, Daventry (01327 702010) – *Indian*
- Paradise Pizzas, Daventry (01327 300838) – *pizzas*
- Southam Kitchen, Southam (01926 810168) – *Chinese*
- Shahi, Daventry (01327 702518) – *Indian*
- The Water Margin, Daventry (01327 312600) – *Chinese*

SLEEPING

Daventry's growing status as a business location has meant the development of some large hotels around the town. Equally, Southam has a couple of smaller hotels and Braunston's Manor is now also a hotel. More basic options are thin on the ground, which may mean that this section is probably best passed through rather than stayed in if budgets are tight.

HOTELS

- Braunston Manor Hotel, Braunston (01788 890267) – *400-year-old property with 7 bedrooms*
- The Daventry Hotel, Daventry (01327 307000) – *modern hotel by Daventry Water*
- Hanover International Hotel and Club, Daventry (01327 307000)
- The Stoneythorpe Hotel, Southam (01926 812365) – *23 bedrooms*
- The Tarsus Hotel, Southam, Daventry Road (Daventry Road 01926 813585) – *Greek and Turkish restaurant with 12 hotel rooms*

BED AND BREAKFAST/GUEST HOUSES

- Abercorn Hotel, Daventry (01327 703741)
- Briarwood, Warwick Road, Southam (01926 814756)
- Burnt Walls Guest House, Daventry (01327 706043)
- Daventry Lodge Farm House, B&B, Daventry (01327 876365)
- Kingsthorpe Guest House, Daventry (01327 702752)
- The Old Bakery, Southam (01926 813225)
- Three Ways B&B, Daventry (01327 361631)

CAMPING

There are two campsites in this section, although camping and caravanning is also offered by the house at Napton Junction (01296 810303). The two sites are:

- NG Adkins, Holt Farm, Southam (01926 812225) – *45 motorhome/ caravan/tent pitches. Free fishing for campers.*
- Woodbine Farm, Grandborough Fields (01788 810349)

In addition, Caravan Club members may try Braunston Marina (01788 891373), where there is a site with five pitches.

Unfortunately, there are no outlets selling camping equipment in this section.

Braunston Turn.

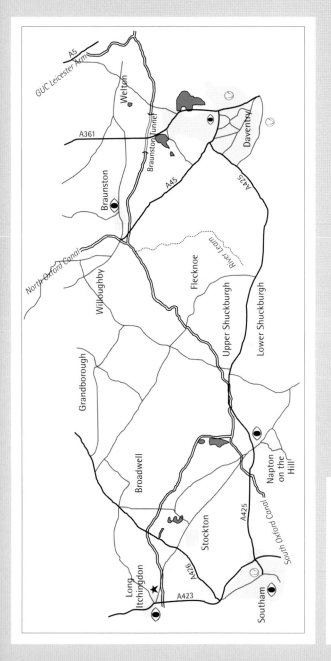

Key

═══════	Canal
··············	River
⊥⊥⊥⊥⊥⊥	Railway
─ ─ ─	Motorway
────────	A Road
────────	B Road
🟤	Built up area
●	Stations
🔴	Open water
◉	Site/Sight
○	Leisure
★	Entertainment
🏛	Culture

SEEING AND DOING

INTRODUCTION

There are some sights worth seeing along this section, although you have to seek them out a little. Little Itchington and Braunston are convenient for the towpath but otherwise cultural sustenance tends to involve a diversion. In line with developments generally, Daventry used to have a Tourist Information Centre, but this is now closed.

SIGHTS

It is worth pulling off the towpath briefly to investigate Long Itchington, if for nothing else simply to absorb the sense of this being a quintessential English village, the stuff of 1950s films, with its village pond, half-timbered houses – especially the Tudor House on the main road – and its pubs. It also has a church, Holy Trinity, which is worth pausing at and gazing upwards in order to see if you can make out the stump of a spire erected in 1762 when the original fell victim to a gale.

Outside Long Itchington there is also a model village, although not one with miniature people. This charming development was built to house workers at the local cement works and sits alongside the disused railway.

Having gained its charter as early as the thirteenth century, and given its position on the east–west drovers' road as well as the road linking Welsh markets to the Midlands, Southam has enjoyed a long history, many remnants of which remain today.

Of particular interest is the 'Halliwell', now known as the Holywell, the water from which was said to cure eye ailments. Water from this and other wells continued to supply the town until the mains came in the 1920s. In fact, Southam has something of a pedigree in medical matters, having played host to the first free Provident Dispensary, established in 1818 by local surgeon Henry Lilley-Smith, who also founded an Eye and Ear Infirmary in what is now the Stoneythorpe Hotel.

> On the edge of Southam is Dallas Burston Polo Grounds, the home of the Royal Leamington Spa Polo Club.

As might be expected, given that Southam was once owned by Coventry Priory, the town's main church, St James, also has a long history, having been founded in 1294. It is notable both for its windows, which cover a range of styles, and its carvings, which include four green men.

The chemist's shop in Southam's High Street was once the Manor House where King Charles I rested shortly, along with his son the Prince of Wales, and James, the Duke of York. With them as their tutor was Dr William Harvey, later to become famous as the man who discovered the circulation of blood. The Olde Mint pub, an imposing stone edifice dating back to the fourteenth century, was where Charles I is thought to have minted coins for his troops.

Napton is dominated by its iconic windmill, which lords itself over the village from the hill. This dates back to 1543, although the current structure

SECTION D

> There were originally two Napton windmills. The current survivor lost two sails in a gale in 1976.

was built around 1835, with some of the buildings surrounding it added in 1910. The mill has good stone foundations and is made of tarred red brick. Although it is not possible to visit the mill, a footpath goes all the way to the entrance of the house before passing to the right.

This is worth following for two reasons. The first is the view just after the house, which allows the visitor to pick out the course of the South Oxford Canal; the second is the double-backed seat hidden away on the right on the road going up to the windmill. This was established on the fiftieth anniversary of the Blitz, alongside a Rowan tree, and marks the site of a look-out post from which the bombing of Coventry was witnessed by a team of powerless observers.

Where the road bends you can cut through some trees to St Lawrence's church. The church has painted copies of records of donations to the poor dating back to 1816, including £50 left by Mr Henry Bates for equal division between twenty poor widows on St Thomas' Day in 1844.

Braunston is also worth pausing in, both down on the canal where there is the marina and the Stop House, used to collect tolls from the stop lock that was once here, and in the village itself. Here the large All Saint's church opposite the Manor House sits at one end of the main street. Not that old, being built in 1849, this is the third church on the site and retains its Norman font. Its 150ft-spire dominates the views from miles around.

It is possible to pick up a leaflet with a series of circular walks around Braunston from the shop, and these highlight features such as The Old Bakery which is easily identified by its old Hovis sign outside, and a cruck-style house once lived in by a family

> Braunston's windmill was once the scene of a terrible accident when the wind turned one of the sails where a workman was carrying out some maintenance, leading him to fall to his death.

Braunston turn from the top.

who ground their own corn at the nearby windmill. There is also the Old Forge on the High Street, where it is possible to see a bricked-up coal chute on the side wall, and the windmill, now a private residence.

Little tangible evidence remains of Daventry's past. Even its small museum, which focused on the Civil War Battle of Naseby, closed recently, and the BBC transmitter which for many is forever linked with the name of Daventry, has gone. Although at one time the home of a Cluniac order of monks, whose monastery sat next to the parish church, nothing remains of this either. The church itself was replaced in 1758 by today's Holy Cross church, built of local ironstone. The impressive Market Cross at the end of the High Street is perhaps the town's most distinguishing feature.

Otherwise, perhaps Daventry's greatest asset these days is the Country Park sited next to the reservoir, itself a feeder for the canal. This covers 140 acres through which there are circular walks, an adventure playground, an interpretation centre, bird-watching hides and picnic areas.

CULTURE AND ENTERTAINMENT

This is not an area alive with cultural and entertainment possibilities. Daventry used to have a cinema but, like so much else in this town, it is no more. There are two art galleries in the town, the Evergreen (01327 878117) and Tribute Pictures (01327 311600), although they do not constitute reason for a detour.

Napton plays host to an annual boat gathering, normally held over the third weekend in September at the Top Lock on the South Oxford Canal, with a barbeque, music, auction and a quiz night. Live music can also be heard at the Two Boats at Long Itchington on a Saturday night and at the Abercorn Hotel in Daventry (see 'Basics').

Southam has a leisure centre with swimming pool (01926 817788) and Daventry has a leisure centre and an outdoor pool (01327 300001). The former (01327 871144) has a 25m indoor pool with a wave machine and water cannons, as well as a fitness club and sport hall. Also in Daventry is the Sports Park (01327 300001), a complex comprising artificial sports surfaces and grass pitches.

Nightlife is concentrated in Daventry where there are a couple of clubs, although names are subject to change:

- Madison Nightclub and Freddies Bar (01327 300288)
- Square (formerly Embryo) (01327 301301)

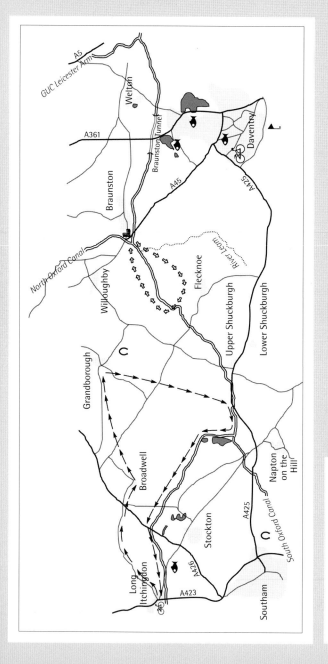

Key

	Canal
	River
	Railway
	Motorway
	A Road
	B Road
	Built up area
	Stations
	Open water
	Cycling route/outlet
	Walking route/outlet
	Fishing spot/outlet
	Golf course/outlet
	Riding outlet

SAMPLING

INTRODUCTION

Despite its wide open spaces, this can be a difficult area to sample properly, due in part to the large prairie-like fields that cover so much of it. It is possible to explore, although it's best to plan your routes beforehand. The area is covered in its entirety by OS Explorer Map 222 Rugby and Daventry.

WALKING

Other than the towpath, the main formal walking route along this section is the Jurassic Way, which follows the limestone ridge across the northern portion of Northamptonshire and passes through Braunston. Less formal walking is available in Daventry Country Park to the west of Daventry Reservoir, where there is also parking.

> An annual tradition of wassailing is upheld in Daventry Country Park each January, when the orchard trees are 'woken up' for the spring with a mixture of noise and morris dancing, accompanied by a large bonfire and apple-based refreshments.

Otherwise, this is not an area rich in footpaths, although it is possible to follow routes across fields, heading generally in a north-easterly direction from the towpath. The countryside is peppered with abandoned medieval villages and Walk D takes the opportunity to explore two of these while also offering a chance to sample the canal at Braunston.

SECTION D

Braunston Marina.

SECTION D WALK
The Medieval Villages of Wolfhampcote and Braunstonbury

Description:	*Some hills, but otherwise country tracks and roads with some spectacular views.*
Distance:	*4.5 miles*
Duration:	*1.5 hours*
Starting point:	*Grid Reference 535659, OS Explorer 222*
Nearest refreshment:	*The Old Olive Bush, Flecknoe*

Start on the western side of Bridge 91 and walk along the track heading south and follow the fingerpost signed to Wolfhampcote Church. Continue along the track as it bends to the right, ignoring the Private Road sign (this is a public footpath) until you reach the church. Now abandoned, this is currently in the care of the Churches Conservation Trust. Along the way there is clear evidence of ridge and furrow farming, as well as the old medieval villages of Wolfhampcote and Braunstonbury.

Continue on the road past a hall and pick up the unclassified road on your left. This goes past an old railway embankment and just at the point that it curves to the left, pick up the footpath on your right, sticking to the left-hand boundary of a field. Just as the hedgerow runs out on the crest of the hill, follow the path to your left, aiming for a gap in the hedge in front of you.

The path continues its direction over the following field. Cross over a stile and head slightly more to the right past a pond, over another stile and then sharp left onto a road. Turn right here and pick up the track on the right past a barn. This takes you down a steep hill and a canal bridge (No.101) soon hoves into view. Pick up the footpath on the opposite side and follow this back to Braunston, bearing right at the double bridges at the Turn.

There are no walking equipment outlets along this section.

CYCLING

Most country roads are concentrated to the north of this section, and the Warwickshire Feldon Cycleway cuts across the towpath at Bridge 18, utilising local bridleways. Other bridleways are scattered around the section (see 'Riding') and also provide good surfaces for riding. As remarked upon elsewhere, however, the towpath after Napton Junction can be decidedly uneven and narrow, and is probably best avoided.

A good way to sample this section on two wheels is by beginning in Long Itchington and heading north along Collingham Lane, which you pick up at the three-way junction with Stockton Road and the A423. Stick with this over a crossroads and sharp bends to the right, as well as over the A426, and then follow it left into Broadwell. In the heart of the village take the turn to the left and follow this to a T-junction, where you head straight ahead, using a bridle-way, turning right on reaching the road and heading into Grandborough.

Take the road on the right just before entering the village and head south-west until you reach another T-junction, where you again go straight ahead onto a bridleway. Follow this for the best part of two miles before reaching a junction of paths, where you head right. This brings you past Ventnor Farm and a road where you turn left and soon join the towpath where you head north-west as far as Bridge 23. Upon reaching this, head right back to your starting point, completing a total of around thirteen, predominately flat, miles.

Cycle outlets along this section include:

- Daventry Cycle Centre, Daventry (01327 310333)
- Leisure Lakes Cycles, Daventry (01327 310400)

RIDING

Along bridleway links Southam to Broadwell, crossing over the towpath at Bridge 18, and this forms part of the Feldon Way. Similarly, a combination of bridleways and roads link this same bridge with Lower Shuckburgh and Grandborough. The latter is used in the cycle route described above, while the former can be combined with the towpath to head all the way to above the Braunston Tunnel via Flecknoe by way of a bridleway leaving the canal east at Bridge 103.

Other stretches of bridleway also exist, heading north out of Long Itchington and following the path of the River Leam south of Braunston, and along the Jurassic Way.

Horse-riding establishments and outlets along this section include:

- A & J Saddlery, Southam (01926 812238)
- Woodbine Farm, Grandborough Fields (01788 810349) – *livery*

FISHING

The best fishing along this stretch is from local reservoirs, although the stretch of canal around Shuckburgh is run by the Coventry and District AA, and Braunston AC (01788 891938) controls the run from Braunston Turn to the tunnel which offers bream and roach.

British Waterways run the Stockton Reservoir (01564 784634), which has sixty-six pegs. No longer used to supply the canal, this is situated behind the Blue Lias pub in Long Itchington, and offers constant water and a pleasant environment with reed beds and an island. A mixed fishery, Stockton has tench, crucian carp, chub, rudd and roach, with some of the carp reaching double figures.

The two Daventry reservoirs are also good spots, with boardwalks stretching out along the water. Drayton Reservoir (01132 816895) to the north of the town and just below Braunston Tunnel is reckoned by many to be among the

SECTION D

best match fisheries in the country, and in 2004 yielded its first 40lb carp. So good is the fishing here that British Waterways suggests two keep nets for keeping perch, roach and tench. There is also a monthly pike match from November through to March here.

Daventry Reservoir (01327 877193) is less spectacular and the best bet for fishing here is to get in touch with Daventry AC. Bream, crucian carp, perch, pike, roach, rudd and tench are all available from the East Bay.

Outlets selling fishing supplies along this stretch include:
• Fishy Business, Daventry (01327872175)

OTHER

This stretch is not that well provided for with other ways of sampling, although there is one full golf course and a municipal pitch and putt:

• Daventry and District, Daventry (01327 702829) – *shortish (5,812 yards) course with undulating ground and short greens*

• Daventry Pitch and Putt (01327 300001) – *municipal par-3 course*

There is also canoeing on both Drayton and Daventry Reservoirs.

Long Itchingdon's truncated church spire.

SECTION E
NORTON JUNCTION TO BLISWORTH

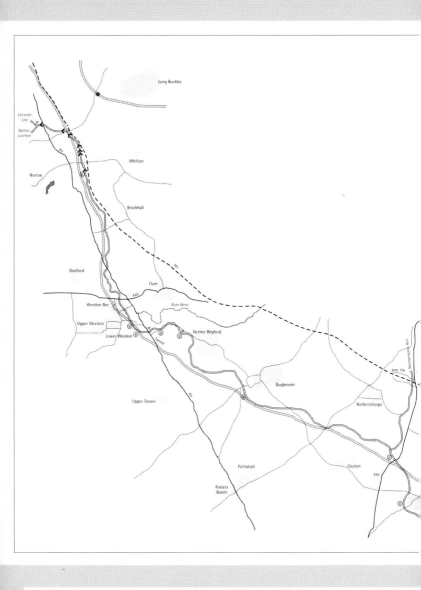

Long Buckby

Leicester
Line

Norton
Junction

Norton

Whilton

Brockhall

Dodford

Flore

Weedon Bec

Upper Weedon

Lower Weedon

Nether Heyford

Bugbrooke

Upper Stowe

Rothersthorpe

Gayton

Pattishall

Fosters
Booth

River Nene

M1

A5

A45

Junc 15a

A43

Northampton Arm

Key

═══ Canal	⬤ Built up area	◯ Turning point
·········· River	⬤ Stations	⌃ Lock
⊞⊞⊞ Railway	⬤ Open water	Ⓑ Boatyard
─ ─ ─ Motorway		W Waterpoint
─── A Road		
─── B Road		

SHAPERS

THE CANAL ON THIS STRETCH

KEY FACTS

LENGTH: 12 miles

BOATYARDS: 9

Whilton Marina
Waterways Services, Weedon
Millar Marine, Weedon
Stowe Hill Wharf
High House Wharf, Nether Heyford
Bugbrooke Wharf
Millar Marine, WeedonGayton Marina (Northampton Arm)
Grand Junction Boat Co., Blisworth Junction
Blisworth Tunnel Boats

WATERPOINTS: 4

Norton Junction
Lower Weedon
Bridge 29
Gayton Junction

TURNING POINTS: 7

Norton Junction
Bridge 15
Bridge 28
Furnace Wharf
Bugbrooke Wharf
Bridge 47
Gayton Junction

LOCKS: 7

Buckby Flight (7) (63ft)

This is a pleasant rural stretch that starts with a short flight of locks and, with the singular exception of Weedon, then seems to make every effort to avoid the various Northamptonshire villages nearby, before ending with a certain finality at Blisworth Tunnel. Roads and railway weave around the towpath throughout.

Norton Junction starts with a run of moorings and a waterpoint, with the towpath extending either side of the water until the beginning of a seven-lock flight, the only locks on this section.

The canal passes under the A5 after the first lock, following which there is a short gap before the flight gets going in earnest. After this the locks are closer, but are never

Anchor Cottage (01327 842140), in the gap between the first two locks, sells a variety of canalia and crafts, as well as ice creams in the summer.

packed in tight. The canal passes under a series of bridges, including one carrying the railway as it passes through the locks and the motorway comes alongside from the left.

Whilton Marina, the first of several along this stretch, is an impressive sight at the bottom of the locks with its huge capacity. There is also a chandlery and shop here. After the locks there is a run of temporary moorings and a long, straight section leading up to Bridge 18, with the canal sitting between the M1 and the railway, with the latter perched up on an embankment.

The motorway curves away to the left after Bridge 19 where the canal takes a distinct southward dive heading for Bridge 21, after which it wriggles a little on its way down to Weedon. The A5 crosses over at Bridge 22 and the railway almost touches the canal on the penultimate bend before Weedon. The towpath becomes more enclosed here, with high trees either side, as well as more solid after a fairly bumpy section following the locks.

A short run of fourteen-day moorings announces Weedon, which is quickly passed through, with Weedon Wharf marking the fact that you have emerged at the other side. It is possible to turn here and to take on water shortly after. Boaters will find progress slow here as there is a long run of moored boats on the non-towpath side, but there is some pretty scenery to distract the attention. Mooring is also possible on the towpath and it is no surprise that this can be a popular spot.

The A5 crosses back over and is followed shortly afterwards by Stowe Hill Wharf and its boatyard. The railway, meanwhile, heads over to the right to pass through Stowe Hill Tunnel. The views now develop further, looking out onto rolling hills and countryside. There is another turning point here and yet another boatyard at High House Wharf outside Nether Heyford, with the village itself accessible from either Bridge 29 or 32.

The canal diverts to the east, approaching Nether Heyford, and it is easy to see the reasons why in the landscape: with a depression to the left, the canal is quite clearly following the base of a small hill. The canal body swerves the village, after which it is again possible to turn, and there is a further long line of moored boats here.

The railway reappears just as the canal enters a long straight up to Bridge 34, after which it bends sharply right to sweep along the southern edge of Bugbrooke. The towpath loses some of its previous good definition for a while, although it improves markedly after Bridge 35 and the run in to Bugbrooke Wharf, with its pub, turning point (60ft at the most) and boatyard.

This long sweep to the south of Bugbrooke continues all the way up to Banbury Lane Bridge (No.3) and although the railway once again makes its presence known, there are also some good views out onto the Bugbrooke Downs to the right, with Gayton sitting on top of a small hill.

After this a long straight with a slight kink in it takes you up to turnover bridge No.47, after which the towpath extends to both sides of the canal down to Gayton Junction. This stretch is occupied by long-term moorings on either side and a boatyard tucked away a short distance up the Northampton Arm. There is also a waterpoint.

The towpath crosses back over to the left at Bridge 48 just after the junction by some pretty cottages, after which there is a run of visitors' moorings. The canal passes under the A43 and soon resumes its previous pattern before coming into Blisworth, one of the few villages along this section that actually sits on the canal. Here you are greeted with yet another boatyard and a spectacular five-storey warehouse on the water's edge.

Quite naturally, boaters find this an agreeable spot to moor although the water can be shallow in places. The

> One of the longest in the country, Blisworth Tunnel celebrated its bicentenary in 2005. It was so delayed that for five years boat cargoes had to be lifted and taken over the top of the hill by horse.

tunnel which made Blisworth famous is a long time coming and is unassuming when reached. At this point non-boaters have to follow the signs up and over the tunnel to follow 1.5-mile footpath alongside Stoke Road to reach the southern portal.

PRINCIPAL TOWNS AND VILLAGES ALONG THIS STRETCH

BLISWORTH:
Although largely overshadowed in canal terms by Stoke Bruerne, Blisworth is a highly attractive village in its own right, with some pretty stone buildings, many of them thatched.

BUGBROOKE:
Bugbrooke was Northamptonshire Village of the Year in 2004, although it can feel more like an elegant small town. The centre has been eroded away over the years, leaving a small village green on the High Street, but plenty of older properties remain.

BROCKHALL:
An isolated hamlet typical of the area with the church, manor house and a farm clustered close together to form a centre.

DODFORD:
A quiet village with an interesting Manor House and a small stream, a mile outside of Weedon.

FLORE:
With a main street of mainly thatched cottages, Flore sits on the A45, a position it exploits by having two pubs.

FOSTERS BOOTH:
A collection of houses either side of the A5 most notable for its pub and restaurant.

GAYTON:
A deceptively large village on a hill with some interesting houses, the occasional grandeur of which is contrasted by the prefabricated village hall.

LONG BUCKBY:

A pleasing mix of housing styles with Victorian and Edwardian terraces existing side by side with more modern developments and old thatched and ivy-clad farm houses. These days it is mainly a commuter village for nearby Northampton.

NETHER HEYFORD:

A compact village with a large green and school at its centre, Nether Heyford has grown successfully over the years and has retained a good sense of community spirit.

NORTON:

A small village strung out along a busy minor road. Its main feature is a pub in its centre with a mature monkey-puzzle tree out front.

PATTISHALL:

Just off the A5, the older part of Pattishall is clustered around its church and a small triangular green, and merges into nearby Fosters Booth.

ROTHERSTHORPE:

A sleepy village with a large manor house at its heart, sited away from the main road. Look out for the large dovecote in North Street.

UPPER STOWE:

Linked with nearby Church Stowe in the Stowe Nine Churches Parish, Upper Stowe nestles among the rolling hills round about. It is a charming collection of Northamptonshire stone cottages with a small green where there is an unusual Millennium bench around a tree.

WEEDON:

Taking in Upper and Lower Weedon and Weedon Bec, Weedon combines the three transport throughfares of

The 'Bec' in Weedon Bec is due to links with the Abbey of Bec Hellonin in France.

the A5, which meets the A45 here: the canal and the railway, with a large viaduct carrying the latter through the village. Lower Weedon is more picturesque with its church and stone cottages, while Weedon Bec is mostly pubs and hotels with a large development of houses hidden away on the hillside.

WHILTON:

Not to be confused with Whilton Locks, which is a collection of businesses and shops down by the canal, Whilton is a pleasant collection of houses built of Northamptonshire stone, lacking an obvious centre. The village's most notable feature is the strange extension to St Andrew's church.

HISTORY

Although evidence has been found of Roman occupation along this stretch, the villages strung out along it are more likely to be Saxon in origin, with some significant enough to appear in the Domesday Book. Villages are what they have remained, however, with none really having gained so much as town status. Long Buckby showed promise at one point when in 1281 its Lord of the Manor, Henry de Lacy, won the right from the king to hold a weekly market and two annual fairs, but contrary to the experience elsewhere, this did not act as a catalyst to growth as a market town.

The countryside along this stretch is sometimes known as the heart of England, although it is possibly a little too far south for this to be a truly accurate description. It is more likely to have gained this tag through a desire to give it something to distinguish itself, for in reality this is something of a 'nowhere land' between Northampton to the north and Milton Keynes to the south and east.

Wide, flat fields are the main theme, with the rural economy, complete with its swings in fortune, the main determinant of history over the centuries. The most significant Roman settlement along this stretch was probably that at Norton, known as Bannaventa, sitting either side of Watling Street on the modern A5, although a villa has also recently been found at Nether Heyford. Bannaventa was sizeable, with excavations showing an enclosed area of 5.5 hectares and ditch defences which even incorporated towers, although little physical evidence remains today.

After the Romans left, this area became part of the Saxon Kingdom of Mercia, and was recorded as Hamtunscire in the Anglo-Saxon Chronicle of 1011, the prefix 'North' being added to separate the area from the more significant

> Milling continues at Bugbrooke Mill to this day with the Heygates Flour Mill, the Heygate family having farmed in the area since 1562, although they only became involved in milling in the eighteenth century.

South Hamtun on the coast. It was during this time that places such as Blisworth and Bugbrooke began to be established, with the former coming together as a settlement in the Salcey Forest.

Bugbrooke, as its name suggests, owed its existence to a position on a stream, the Hoarestone Brook. By the time of the Norman invasion the mill at Bugbrooke, located by the point where the stream met the River Nene, was deemed to be the third most significant in the country.

> Bugbrooke is also the birthplace of the Jesus Army, an evangelical Christian Church with a charismatic emphasis that grew out of the local Baptist Church in 1970. It now operates in sixty-five churches across the country, and also from community houses.

Other villages developed for different reasons. Brockhall, for example, grew up around Brockhall House, built in 1652 by Edward Eyton and later in the hands of the Thornton family for more than 100 years until the male line died out in 1978. The house is now residential flats. A manor house also explains the existence of Gayton and many of the villages in this section are defined by their local 'big house' and church. Many of these churches were built during the fourteenth and fifteenth centuries, helped by a plentiful supply of stone, and Northamptonshire is sometimes referred to as 'a county of spires', with the spires easily visible across the flat fields.

It was not until the nineteenth century that the outside world really began to intrude on these places, and then only on some. Modern transport systems were to blame, with first the canals and then the railways, and improved roads bringing their force to bear.

Nowhere was this more the case than at Weedon. Sitting in the valley of the River Nene as well as on Watling Street, Weedon attracted not just improved

SECTION E

An indicator of Long Buckby's relative independence from the vicissitudes of the land is its enduring sense of independence. The village founded Northamptonshire's first Co-op, nurtured a strong Chartist movement and was a haven of non-conformist chapels, the combined congregations of which outnumbered the Church of England threefold.

roads in the shape of the modern A5 and A45, but also the canal and a railway line. Although the village's station closed in the 1960s, for eighty years Weedon was the starting point for the branch line to Leamington via Daventry, and the railway continues to run over an impressive viaduct.

The area's reputation for being in the middle of nowhere also came to bear when the decision was made to site a barracks in the town at the height of the Napoleonic Wars. The thinking went that Weedon was a safe bolt-hole, and plans were even laid for the royal family to retreat there in the event of an invasion. A separate arm off the canal's main line was dug, and evidence of this can still be seen today, although the barracks themselves closed in 1965.

Long Buckby also finally took off around this time, although it had enjoyed a century of relative good fortune during the 1700s, when it had been on the edge of the East Anglian clothing industry. This time it was another form of attire, shoes, which provided the wealth. Along with Daventry and Northampton, this trade was to provide a steady income away from the land for many of the local inhabitants, with the canal and its wharf contributing to the village's reputation as an industrial centre.

Once again, though, growth faltered and these days the area's lot seems to be one of a location of sleepy communities content with their existence whatever the centuries contrive to throw at them.

THE NATURAL LANDSCAPE

Although this part of Northamptonshire has a largely justified reputation for being flat and featureless, it is not always the case along this stretch, with both Norton to the north and Gayton and Pattishall to the south sitting on small rises. Flat is the theme for most of the way, though, as demonstrated by the lack of locks along this section.

A number of streams wind their way between fields, but the River Nene flowing through Weedon is by far the most significant natural water. Lakes and reservoirs are conspicuous by their absence, as is woodland, although there is a small wooden section of the towpath west of Brockhall, which itself sits among trees.

ACCESS AND TRANSPORT

ROADS

The M1 cuts a swathe through the heart of this section and has a junction on the eastern edge (15a). The A5, meanwhile, echoes the route of the motorway but to the south, providing a calmer alternative. The A45 also cuts across the section from east to west via Weedon on its way to Junction 16 of the M1, which is just off the map, and the A43 heads south from the M1 and passes to the west of Blisworth. Otherwise, local roads tend to link up with one of the more major trunk roads, with some inter-connecting minor links.

RAIL

Although the railway is a constant presence along this stretch, there are no stations on the main Euston–Birmingham line. The only access by rail is at Long Buckby, which sits on a loop off the main line linking Rugby and Northampton. This is operated by Central Trains (01216 541200). Alternatively, National Train Enquiries can be reached on 08457 484950.

> It was to Long Buckby station that the Prince of Wales and the two princes came when they journeyed to Althorp for the final laying to rest of Princess Diana.

BUSES

The following list sets out the main bus services on this section, although it is advisable to check before using them as some buses only run on certain days and others may have been withdrawn since publication of this Guide.

- 40/41 – *Northampton to Daventry via Bugbrooke, Nether Heyford and Flore (UC)*
- 86/87 – *Northampton circular via Pattisall and Rothersthorpe (MK Metro)*
- 96 – *Daventry to Long Buckby (UC)*
- G1 – *Norton to Northampton via Whilton (SMS)*
- X42 – *Northampton to Daventry via Flore (UC)*

In addition, Northants County Council runs a Gayton and Tiffield Community minibus into Towcester on Tuesdays and Fridays.

Contact details for bus operators in this area are listed below, although Traveline (www.traveline.org.uk) on 0870 6082608 can give details of specific services between 7 a.m. and 10 pm.:

- MK Metro, Milton Keynes (01908 668366)
- SMS, Towcester (01327 353118)
- United Counties, Northampton (01604 601502)

TAXIS

The following list gives a selection of the taxi operators in this section:

- Artisan Private Hire, Nether Heyford (01327 341418)
- Buckby Cab Company, Long Buckby (01327 844589)
- The Village Shuttle, Long Buckby (01327 842961)

The gate to the Royal Ordnance depot at Weedon.

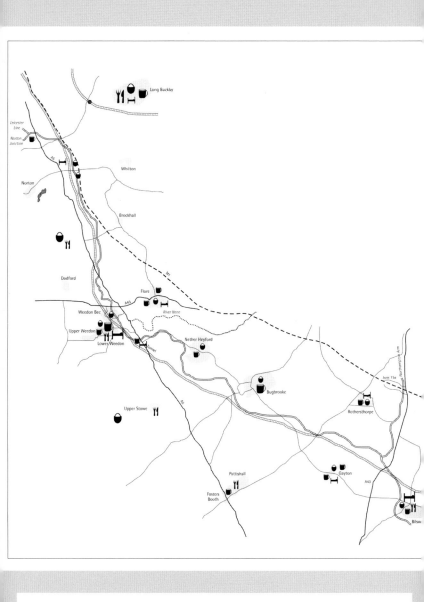

Long Buckby

Leicester Line

Norton Junction

Whilton

Norton

Brockhall

Dodford

Flore

Weedon Bec

Upper Weedon

Lower Weedon

River Nene

Nether Heyford

Upper Stowe

Bugbrooke

Rothersthorpe

Northampton Arm

June 15a

Gayton

A43

Pattishall

Fosters Booth

Bilsw

Key

Canal	⬤ Built up area	Shops
River	● Stations	Accomodation
Railway	● Open water	Campsite
Motorway		Pub
A Road		Restaurant
B Road		

BASICS

INTRODUCTION

Not even its biggest fans could call this a busy stretch of the canal, more of a run to be got through (or savoured!) before the delights of Milton Keynes. It should not be simply dismissed, however, as the area is scattered with villages where it is possible to make a serendipitous discovery by way of a farm shop, high-quality restaurant or, perhaps most likely, a friendly welcome and a delicious pint in one of the pubs that dot the route.

SHOPPING

Supplies need a bit of planning along this stretch, with shops at a premium, especially canalside, although there are some surprises along the way. Some way off the towpath, Long Buckby probably has the most comprehensive range of shops including a hardware store (which also sells fishing tackle), a newsagents, a pharmacy and a post office. In addition, the village has two supermarkets, a Co-op and a Costcutter as well as a WI Market on Thursday mornings.

Anchor Cottage on the towpath by the locks sells canal related giftware, while the Garden Centre on the other side of the locks may also be useful for the odd item. Perhaps the most useful shop in these parts is Sunny Meadow Farm by the wharf which sells free-range eggs and home-grown vegetables in season, which says much for the restricted range of what is on offer.

The next place offering any kind of supplies is Weedon, although Weedon Bec close to the canal is more of an antiques centre than a High Street. Towpath travellers will need to walk up to Lower Weedon for anything more substantial, where there is a post office, pharmacy and newsagent.

Weedon does, however, boast a couple of retail centres nearby. The first of these is the Heart of the Shires (01327 349249) located among some farm buildings dating back to the mid-nineteenth century, just off the A5 between Weedon and Norton. This 'shopping village' has a range of specialist outlets selling items from lingerie, African arts and crafts to cookware, and also has a corner specialising in pickles.

The second is the Old Dairy Farm Craft Centre (01327 340525) in Upper Stowe which is also sited among Victorian buildings and has a number of craft shops, a delicatessen and bookshop, as well as being home to the Barnyard restaurant (see 'Eating').

There is a newsagent in Flore, but Nether Heyford is more promising with a newsagent of its own, a Costcutter, a butchers and a patisserie. Bugbrooke boasts a newsagent and off-licence as well as a handful of more specialist shops and a smaller post office.

It can be worth stopping off in Rothersthorpe to visit the Polebarn Farm Shop near the village hall, while Gayton has a post office and a small village stores. Finally, Blisworth has both the Blisworth News and Blisworth Post Office and Stores just off Bridge 50.

EATING AND DRINKING

There is a reasonable variety of pubs along this section, with Long Buckby and Weedon providing the greatest concentrations, although Flore and Bugbrooke also boast more than one.

PUBS

- The Admiral Rodney, Long Buckby (01327 844144)
- The New Inn, Long Buckby (01327 844747)
- The Peacock, Long Buckby (01327 843172)
- Old King's Head, Long Buckby (01327 844195)
- The New Inn, Buckby Wharf (01327 842540) – *by Buckby Top Lock at Bridge 11*
- The Royal Oak, Flore (01327 341340)
- The White Hart, Flore (01327 341580)
- Red Lion, Fosters Booth (01327 830259)
- The Heart of England, Weedon (01327 340335)
- The Crossroads, Weedon Bec (01327 340354)
- The Wheatsheaf, Weedon Bec (01327 340670)
- Plume of Feathers, Lower Weedon (01327 340978)
- The Narrow Boat, Stowe Hill Wharf (01327 340536)
- The Foresters Arms, Nether Heyford (01327 340622)
- The Bakers Arms, Bugbrooke (01604 830865)
- The Five Bells, Bugbrooke (01604 832483)
- The Wharf Inn, Bugbrooke (01604 832585)
- The Chequers, Rothersthorpe (01604 830892)
- The Eykyn Arms, Gayton (01604 858361)
- The Queen Victoria, Gayton (01604 858878)
- The Royal Oak, Blisworth (01274 858372)

EATING

Generally, the best places to eat along this stretch are the many pubs, although there are one or two specialist restaurants scattered around in between the usual takeaways and Asian dining experiences – although fish and chips are thin on the ground. The following represents a selection of restaurants along this section:

- The Barn Restaurant, Upper Stowe (01327 349911) – *English*
- The Big Fryer, Long Buckby (01327 842807) – *fish and chips*
- The Blisworth Coaching Inn, Blisworth (01604 859551) – *English*
- The Crossroads, Weedon Bec (01327 340354) – *Chef and Brewer*
- Darlington Tea Rooms, Heart of the Shires Shopping Village, Weedon (01327 342284)
- The Dynasty, Long Buckby (01327 842007) – *Chinese*
- Four Pillars Restaurant, Fosters Booth (01327 830391) – *Indian*
- Glenmore House, Long Buckby (01327 844179) – *Mediterranean*
- Lucky House, Long Buckby (01327 349363) – *Chinese*
- Village Garden, Long Buckby (01327 844804) – *Indian*
- Voujon, Long Buckby (01327 843571) – *Indian*
- Weedon House, Weedon (01327 349388) – *Chinese*
- Whilton Locks Garden Centre (01327 843100) – *canalside 'lite bites'*

Outside Nether Heyford.

SLEEPING

Weedon's position at the junction of the A5 and A45 has resulted in a number of hotels, while its proximity to Silverstone, home of the British Grand Prix, also helps to support a wider spread of places to stay than might otherwise be expected.

HOTELS

- Courtyard by Marriott, Flore (01327 349022) – *53 rooms, modern hotel*
- The Crossroads, Weedon Bec (01327 340354) – *Premier Inn*
- The Globe, Weedon Bec (0845 4566399) – *18 rooms in an old coaching inn*
- The Heart of England, Weedon (01327 340335) – *canalside*
- The Walnut Tree Inn, Blisworth (01604 859551) – *200 yards from the canal*

BED AND BREAKFAST/GUEST HOUSES

- The Haven, Rothersthorpe (01604 830621)
- Grafton Villa, Blisworth (01604 858104)
- Little Lodge, Ravensthorpe (01604 770014)
- Murcott Mill, Long Buckby (01327 842236) – *farmhouse B&B*
- The Narrow Boat, Stowe Hill Wharf (01327 340536)
- Queen Victoria, Gayton (01604 858878) – *pub with 4 rooms*
- Sunny Meadow Farm, Long Buckby Wharf (01327 842574) – *canalside*

CAMPING
This section is something of a desert for camping, with no recognised sites and nowhere to top up supplies.

SECTION E

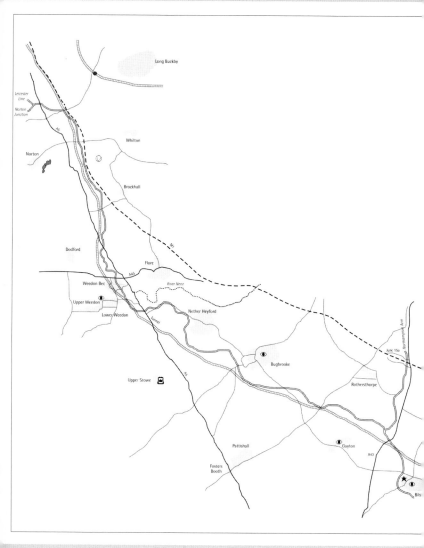

Long Buckby

Leicester Line

Norton Junction

Whilton

Norton

Brockhall

Dodford

Flore

Weedon Bec

Upper Weedon

River Nene

Lower Weedon

Nether Heyford

Tunnel

Upper Stowe

Bugbrooke

Rothersthorpe

Northampton Arm

June 15a

Pattishall

Gayton

A43

Fosters Booth

Bils

Key

══════ Canal	● Built up area	◉ Site/Sight	
········· River	● Stations	⊘ Leisure	
▥▥▥▥ Railway	● Open water	★ Entertainment	
─ ─ ─ Motorway		⊞ Culture	
────── A Road			
────── B Road			

SEEING AND DOING

INTRODUCTION

This section's attractions are generally subtle rather than grandiose, with the delight often lying in the detail. Those looking for traditional tourist attractions in the form of theme parks and stately homes must wait – there is no Tourist Information Centre along this stretch for a good reason.

As highlighted in 'Shapers', many of the villages along this stretch have been defined by the local 'big house' and church, and there are plenty of opportunities to see evidence of this along this section. In most cases the best bet is probably to devise your own walk through the villages as none have so much as a published trail (although some are planning to address this), using the highlights described below as a starting point.

SIGHTS

Before venturing away from the towpath it is worth remembering that the canal itself is a sight worth absorbing along this section, notably Norton and Gayton Junctions and the locks to the north, bounded as they are by one of the country's largest marinas.

> When the railway came, it cut across the canal link to the Ordnance depot, which meant that a portion of the line had to be removed each time barges loaded with gunpowder came with a fresh delivery. The sheer danger involved with this was one of the contributing factors to the depot's eventual closure.

Otherwise, the first and grandest sight along this stretch is probably the old Royal Ordnance Depot at Weedon, which can be viewed, but alas, not visited. Not sitting by the canal, this is easily missed. Those curious to view it need to head for Lower Weedon and find the school, which leads to Ordnance Lane.

Commissioned in 1803, at its height this site covered 150 acres and housed 500 men. Initially, there were eight storehouses covering a distance of a quarter of a mile and four magazines in a walled enclosure, containing 1,000 tons of gunpowder. A separate canal was cut to link the site to the Grand Union, and at each end lodges were built with a moveable portcullis. The canal went actually into the magazine and there was a barge turning area on the other side. Although the high walls and turrets still guarding the depot may be intimidating, the canny may wish to note that Ordnance Lane remains a public footpath after it leaves the road.

Mention has already been made in 'Basics' of the two craft shopping centres/ retail villages to the north of Weedon and in Upper Stowe, which are probably as close as this section gets to formulated tourist attractions.

> Look out for the Millennium Bench wrapped around a tree outside St James' church in Upper Stowe.

Some of the villages described above begin to appear after Weedon. Bugbrooke, for example, which can be reached from Bridge 36, has a church and a Manor Farm, as well as a number

SECTION E

Dodford has one of the longest drive-through fords in the country.

of pubs. It is worth looking out for the sixteenth-century packhorse bridge here which passes over a small tributary of the Nene. There is also a seventeenth-century Quaker's Meeting House still in the village (although it is now a private residence) as well, of course, as the church – St Michael and All Angels.

Gayton is also worth wandering around. The village still has its Tudor Manor, built by Sir Francis Tanfield, and is opposite the church of St Mary's, which is open to visitors. Gayton sits on the junction of five routes and has a small green at the point where they all come together, recently adorned with a colourful new sign.

Almost certainly, Blisworth will be the name that chimes most with towpath travellers, not least because of its famous tunnel. Although it gave its name to this feature of the canal, the village has become somewhat overshadowed in recent times by Stoke Bruerne on the other side of the bore, which is a shame as the village has much to offer.

Blisworth definitely repays a short stroll, with many of its buildings distinctive in that they are constructed in bands of Northamptonshire sand-

Blisworth recently won lottery funding to create a Heritage Project to highlight the village's history through a combination of published walks, work with local children and the production of a community play.

stone and local ironstone, making them highly picturesque. Look out also for the Baptist church here as well as the front of Church House, which still has two old insurance plaques on its front.

Blisworth Tunnel was a major feat of engineering at the time of its construction 200 years ago, but completing it was a drawn out affair. Three years into the project the navvies hit quicksand and all work had to be stopped, and a whole new course begun. The tunnel received much needed maintenance work in the 1980s with new concrete sides put in place.

The Corner Cottage, Gayton.

Blisworth Tunnel North Portal.

CULTURE AND ENTERTAINMENT

As might be expected given the shortage of major towns, there are no cinemas, theatres or leisure centres in the villages covered in this section. Those seeking cultural or physical sustenance are best advised to head north to Northampton or wait until the delights of Milton Keynes in the next section.

That said, there is a go-karting and off-road driving centre at Whilton Mill (01327 843822) which is popular for corporate hospitality as well as parties.

Upper Stowe has the Small Plaice modern art gallery (01327 344422) which features original paintings and sculpture by Northamptonshire artists, and the Heart of England Shopping Centre has the Rose Gallery.

Finally, the Walnut Tree Inn in Blisworth maintains a tradition of live music that dates back to the 1960s. In the 1970s famous names such as Hawkwind, Deep Purple and Van der Graaf Generator all played here, so it may be worth stopping by to see if you catch some stars of the future – although these days the acts are considerably less sensational!

SECTION E

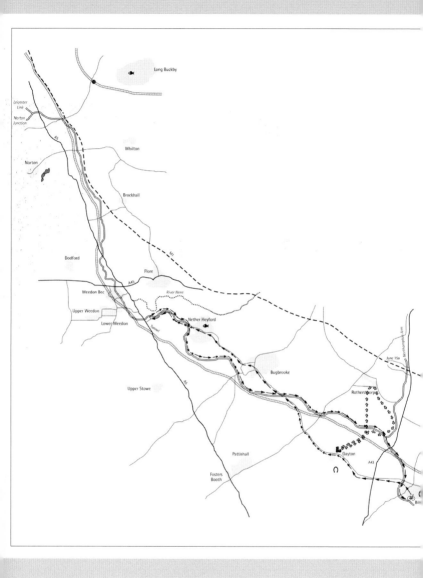

Key

Canal		Built up area		Cycling route/outlet	
River		Stations		Walking route/outlet	
Railway		Open water		Fishing spot/outlet	
Motorway				Golf course/outlet	
A Road				Riding outlet	
B Road					

SAMPLING

INTRODUCTION

The combination of the motorway and railway can intrude on some of the earlier parts of this section, with the latter an almost constant companion all the way through. There are ways of sampling this section away from the towpath, although walking and cycling are probably the best options.

The section is covered by OS Explorer Maps 223, Northampton and Market Harborough and 207, Newport Pagnell and Northampton South.

WALKING

Two formal paths crop up in this section: the Midshires Way, which links the Ridgeway in the Chilterns with the Trans Pennine Trail via the Peak District National Park, and the Nene Way, which follows the Nene Valley from Northamptonshire to the Wash. The first of these joins the section at Weedon and follows a route in the main following minor roads that cuts across the canal at Bridge 41, taking in Nether Heyford, Bugbrooke and Blisworth. The Nene Way cuts through Weedon and heads east.

This is not an area blessed with other walking opportunities, although there are a couple of Sites of Special Scientific Interest. The first of these is Ramsden Corner, west of Upper Stowe, which is rich in grassland including Sheep's Sorrel, the second, Bugbrooke Meadow east of Nether Heyford, a hay meadow with marigolds in early spring.

Walk E starts and finishes in Gayton and takes in both the Grand Union and a part of the Northampton Arm.

Buckby top lock with two boats.

SECTION E WALK
To Rothersthorpe and Back Via Gayton Marina

Description:	*A largely flat walk taking in two canals*
Distance:	*4 miles*
Duration:	*1.5 hours*
Starting point:	*Grid Reference 703547, OS Explorer 207 (W)*
Nearest refreshment:	*The Queen Victoria, Gayton*

Starting in Gayton, pick up the footpath on the right by the church-yard, passing through fields and over first a railway bridge and then another over the canal. Stick with the hedge on your right and, on reaching a copse, bear left to cross a stream. When you get to the field bear right, with the hedge now on your left and cross over two fields.

After a stile head for a white cottage, and then go over another stile into Rothersthorpe. Turn right on the road and then over a stile at a gap in the wall to your right. Cross another field and stream, bearing left to another stile by the road. Keep parallel with the road until you reach a gate and pass through a gap in the fence.

Walk away from the road and over a bridge between two large ponds, and then through a gate and along a wide track. Pick up the towpath on the Northampton Arm and follow it down to Gayton Marina, turning right at the road and onto the Grand Union. Follow this until you reach the bridge you crossed at the beginning of the walk and return to your starting point.

The nearest stockists of walking equipment are in Northampton.

Buckby Locks.

Norton Junction.

CYCLING

The largely flat landscape combined with a reasonable network of minor roads means this section offers good possibilities for exploring by bike. That said, there are a few hills that are probably best avoided and the area is relatively light on other tracks and solid paths. The towpath is in fairly good condition, although it can be narrow at times.

One way to sample this area on two wheels is to start at the parking area by the north portal of the Blisworth tunnel to the south of the village. Turn left out of there and straight ahead at crossroads in the heart of the village, taking the Gayton Road over the A43 and into Gayton itself, turning left to do so. Stick on the Bugbrooke Road into Bugbrooke, crossing the railway and canal and turn left at the far end of the village, following signs to Nether Heyford.

Once in Nether Heyford, follow the road to Weedon which will bring you down to the A5 and Stowehill Wharf. Turn right and pick up the towpath, following this back to Blisworth along a pleasant rural route. This ride is a total of around 17 miles, and is mainly flat, even if the towpath itself can get a little bumpy in places.

Once again, the nearest cycle outlets are in Northampton.

RIDING

Both the Midshires Way and Nene Way provide good opportunities for riding, although the former is mainly road-based. Otherwise, bridleways are restricted to the odd short stretch.

Horse-riding establishments and outlets along this section include:
- Evergreen, Gayton (01604 858247) – *riding school*
- New Tunnel Hill Riding Stables, Blisworth (01604 858041) – *stables*

SECTION E

FISHING

Canal fishing is controlled by a number of different clubs and societies along this stretch, while there are also opportunities for some lake fishing.

- Am Pro, Long Buckby (01327 843091) – *140-peg venue with bream up to 3lb, carp over 10lb, and gudgeon, perch and roach up to 1lb*
- Britannia AC (01604 470190) – *controls fishing at Gayton Junction up the Northampton Arm*
- Daventry AC – *by the locks*
- Flore and Weedon AC – *controls section from Bridge 18 to Bridge 22*

- Northampton Nene AC (01604 762542) – *controls sections from Bridge 22 to Bridge 24, from Bridge 26 to Bridge 47 and from Bridge 48 to Blisworth Tunnel. Tench, bream, perch, roach, carp up to 20lb, pike up to 10lb, eels, ruffe and gudgeon in the section between Bridges 29-32.*

Gayton AC also controls fishing at Gayton Marina where carp over 20lb can be caught. Heyford Fisheries at Nether Heyford (01327 340002) is a manmade canal-type fishery with three lakes: the curving Snake Lake, Acorn Lake set aside for younger anglers, and Carp Lake which is self-explanatory.

Heyford Fisheries came about after the EEC (as it then was) withdrew the agricultural drainage grant which made the land unviable for farming. Instead, the fact that 100,000 gallons of spring water flow through the site every day was turned to an asset in the form of this pleasure fishery.

Outlets selling fishing supplies along this stretch include:

- Bailey's, Long Buckby (01327 842262)
- Trinders Tackle, Nether Heyford (01327 340002)

OTHER

Although Northamptonshire is well provided for with golf courses, none of them lie in this section.

Northampton Arm.

STOKE BRUERNE
TO MILTON KEYNES
(NORTH)

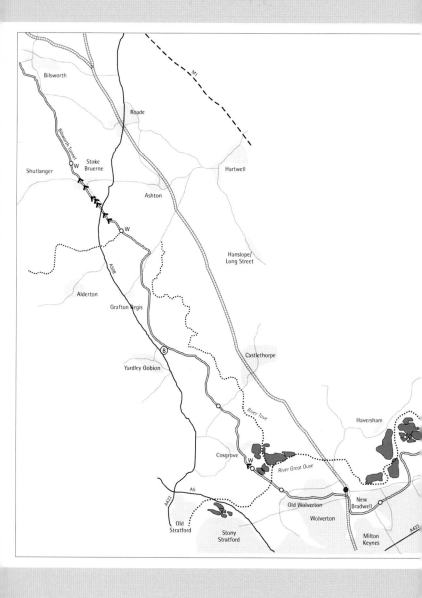

Bilsworth

Roade

M1

Bilsworth Tunnel

Shutlanger

W

Stoke
Bruerne

Hartwell

Ashton

W

A508

Hanslope/
Long Street

Alderton

Grafton Regis

B

Castlethorpe

Yardley Gobion

River Tove

Haversham

Cosgrove

W

River Great Ouse

A5
A422

Old
Stratford

Stony
Stratford

Old Wolverton

Wolverton

New
Bradwell

Milton
Keynes

A422

Key

══════	Canal	⬤ Built up area	◯ Turning point
··········	River	⬤ Stations	⋀ Lock
▥▥▥▥	Railway	⬤ Open water	Ⓑ Boatyard
─ ─ ─	Motorway		W Waterpoint
────	A Road		
────	B Road		

SHAPERS

THE CANAL ON THIS STRETCH

KEY FACTS

LENGTH: 12.5 miles

BOATYARDS: 2
> Baxter Boatfitting, Yardley Gobion
> Cosgrove Marina

WATERPOINTS: 3
> Blisworth Tunnel South Portal
> Bottom of Stoke Bruerne Flight
> Cosgrove Lock

TURNING POINTS: 6
> Blisworth Tunnel South Portal
> Bottom of Stoke Bruerne Flight
> Thrupp Wharf
> Cosgrove
> Old Wolverton
> New Bradwell

LOCKS: 8
> Stoke Bruerne Flight (7) (40ft)
> Cosgrove Lock (3ft 4in)

This is a very pleasant rural stretch book-ended by the Blisworth Tunnel and Stoke Bruerne flight at one end, and the approach to Milton Keynes at the other, where an aqueduct over the Great Ouse provides a dramatic entrance to the city. The towpath varies in quality, being a little bumpy in the middle, but is generally in good condition. Villages exist along the towpath but tend to remain well hidden, with the notable exceptions of Stoke Bruerne and Cosgrove.

As you emerge from the tunnel, glance quickly to the left where there is a concrete section from the middle of the tunnel when it was restored in the 1980s. A winding hole on the right is followed by a long run of visitors' moorings which take you right up to the canal museum and the top lock.

Pass over the top lock and pick up the towpath to the right under the bridge, where almost immediately there is another lock followed by a pound with limited mooring. The main towpath remains on the right although it is possible to travel either side. Three locks follow in quick succession before the bridge carrying the A508, after which there are two more, with the towpath

Do not be alarmed if you see the small nose of a swimming animal protrouding from the water along here – it is likely to be a water vole, not a rat.

switching to the left after the bottom lock, where there is also a waterpoint, sanitary station and, that rare thing on the canal, a recycling point.

It is possible to wind after here where the River Tove joins the canal, with the river acting as a small marina. Ringed visitors' moorings are available here, as the canal adopts a straight course with a good solid towpath passing over a weir where the Tove crosses over to the left.

The views open out here over wide plains and look out to the distant spire of Hanslope church, a landmark which becomes a recurring feature for some miles from now on. A lazy drift towards the left follows, with the river remaining a few feet below to the left. This culminates in a pronounced U-bend swinging the canal over to the right by Bridge 56. After this, the towpath resumes its general southward direction.

The ground rises slightly to the right after Bridge 57, providing a platform for Grafton Regis to gaze down on the scene below. It is possible to moor along most of this stretch, although there is some reinforced banking a short while after the bridge. The path of the Tove on the left can now be traced by rushes lining its bank, and the views remain those of Northamptonshire flatlands.

The towpath becomes decidedly more bumpy along this pleasant rural stretch. Just after a weir, the canal passes to the right and adopts a straight due-south direction punctuated only by Bridge 58 in the middle. Following Bridge 59, the canal sweeps to the left and passes the Baxter Boatyard and marina and the road into Yardley Gobion, which can be accessed from Bridge 60.

Another long, straight section follows, passing through Bridges 61 and 62, with a slight wiggle after the latter. The canal becomes wide and languid at this point, with hedgerows either side. The scenery becomes more colourful with a line of moored boats by Thrupp Wharf where there is a winding hole and a pub by Bridge 64.

The towpath crosses back to the right briefly, after which the water snakes its way down into Cosgrove

The Cosgrove Narrowboat Co. offers boat trips – call 01525 372853.

with the towpath noticeably more solid. The canal sits on a contour here with the surrounding land sloping away gently to the left.

The towpath crosses back over at the magnificent Gothic-style stone-built Soloman's Bridge, shortly after which there is a waterpoint and Cosgrove Marina, as well as plentiful visitors' moorings and another recycling point. Some of the old wharfside buildings have been sympathetically restored and Cosgrove makes for a fine sight on a sunny day.

The relatively long run of lockless water ends at Cosgrove Lock outside the village, a spot which also marks the remnants of where the Buckingham Canal once joined the Grand Union, these days populated with permanent moorings. On the other side of the lock there is a winding hole, one of two either side of the long, straight stretch leading up to the Great Ouse Aqueduct, with the river itself an impressive sight down and to the left.

This long, straight section is always well-populated with boats on both banks, sometimes double-moored, and often acts as a base for a number of historical or unusual craft. The cast-iron aqueduct follows, but is best

Technically, this arm is part of the Old Stratford Arm; 1¼ miles long with no locks, this was completed in 1800.

appreciated from below, although the views either side are worth pausing to appreciate, even if those with vertigo may choose not to pause too long.

A rather unprepossessing sign after the aqueduct welcomes you to Milton Keynes, followed by yet more moorings and a charming canalside cottage by some warehouses and a pub. The bumps in the landscape in the open fields to your left are all that remain of the medieval village of Wolverton.

With the towpath now entering the north-western edge of Milton Keynes, it should come as no surprise that the towpath becomes surfaced. Wolverton is primarily industrial in nature, although a black and white mural depicting various modes of transport leavens the view a little.

The towpath passes by Wolverton station and its twin bridges and swings round to the left. The railway passes overhead once more and the water is restrained by concrete banks as it lines up to pass over another aqueduct, although it in fact goes over a modern road.

A disused windmill sits to the right and the first of the new housing associated with the city begins, adjacent to a modern-looking footbridge, some children's play equipment and a pub on the opposite side. The housing soon fades and this remains a relatively quiet stretch. After Bridge 74 the scenery opens out, with Stantonbury Park Farm to the right and the Linford Lakes to the left.

The canal swings sharply to the right in the midst of this at Bridge 75, a traditional stone affair, just before

> There is more narrowboat day-hire here – call 07721 025325.

which it is possible to see the remains of an old church in the open land to the left. Boats accumulate along the approach to Stantonbury Wharf and Bridge 76, just after which lies the popular Proud Perch pub with its elaborate decking leading down to the canal.

PRINCIPAL TOWNS AND VILLAGES ALONG THIS STRETCH

ALDERTON:
A small hamlet with a collection of thatched cottages clustered around

> Alderton is home to the Rolls Royce Enthusiasts Club.

the church at the northern end with a plant nursery in the middle.

ASHTON:
A small hamlet clustered round its pub, which dates itself back to the 1700s. The village is a collection of mainly well-appointed and recently renovated houses.

CASTLETHORPE:
Perched on the edge of the Tove Valley, the feeling of gentility inspired by half-timbered cottages and red-bricked semis in Castlethorpe is somewhat marred by its proximity to the railway. The village dates back to the times of the Viking invasions, the suffix 'thorpe' being Norse for settlement.

COSGROVE:
A village of two parts with a church and grander building up on the hill and a recently renovated wharfside development on the canal, the two sandwiching

some rather uninspiring modern housing. Cosgrove's highlight is undoubtedly its splendid Gothic bridge over the canal although the village's sign has the church as its chosen motif.

GRAFTON REGIS:

Just tucked off the A508 and a short walk up from the canal, Grafton Regis has managed to retain much of its traditional charm, in particular its combination of manor house, village farm and thirteenth-century church on its northern edge. Elsewhere, thatch is the theme and there is a pub on the nearby main road.

HANSLOPE:

A largely undiscovered gem of a village away from all the main routes. A little probing reveals much history with a church dating back to 1160

> Hanslope's name is derived from the Old English and refers to a muddy slope belonging to someone called Hama.

and a number of interesting buildings, some of which date back to its medieval role as a market town. Hanslope includes the Long Street area to its west.

HARTWELL:

A mixture of housing styles, the oldest buildings dating back to the late seventeenth century being made of coursed rubble limestone. There have been waves of development since, causing today's village to be a collection of estates of various vintages.

HAVERSHAM:

A village of two parts north of Milton Keynes, with the older part to the east consisting of stone-built cottages overlooking the Linford Lakes while the newer part to the west overlooks a railway viaduct and consists of more modern housing.

MILTON KEYNES:

The towpath traveller just gets a taste of Milton Keynes from this section, although the neatness and uniform 'branding' that characterises the city begins to make its presence felt. Trees planted when the city was still a town have now matured and the cycle paths that are something of an icon also begin to appear. Milton Keynes is a love it or loathe it kind of place according to individual taste, and although not every experiment works, it is worth giving it the benefit of the doubt.

NEW BRADWELL:

An outer suburb of Milton Keynes with a parade of shops built originally to house railwaymen from Wolverton, with the Victorian influence on the architecture still evident today.

OLD STRATFORD:

Just over the Great Ouse and therefore the Northamptonshire border, Old Stratford has a large village feel to it with a mix of housing styles.

OLD WOLVERTON:

Old Wolverton calls itself a village but does not feel like one, and is in danger of being swallowed up by industrial estates and its larger neighbour.

The Great Ouse Aqueduct.

ROADE:
Sitting on the busy A508, Roade is split into two parts with one half stretched out along the road and the other, quite distinct, half being much older with thatched cottages, a Victorian primary school and a memorial green.

SHUTLANGER:
Tucked away off the main road, Shutlanger is allied with Stoke Bruerne and exists as a pleasant hamlet which has enjoyed sympathetic modern development. There is a monastery and some attractive cottages sitting on the side of a small stream.

STOKE BRUERNE:
The canal dominates Stoke Bruerne but it is worth peeling away from the towpath to explore this pretty village. The settlement dates back to the Domesday Book and was effectively bisected by the canal, whose engineers chose this spot for the south portal of the Blisworth Tunnel. Today, canal-inspired tourism and the museum are a mainstay of the local economy.

STONY STRATFORD:
Predominately Victorian in appearance, Stony Stratford has an integrity that distinguishes it from nearby Milton Keynes, with a long High Street and a proud history

YARDLEY GOBION:
A walk up the track leading from Baxter's Boatyard, Yardley Gobion is a self-contained village with a triangular green complete with a recently restored village pump. The buildings around the core are of the familiar Northamptonshire stone and thatch, while elsewhere a large modern estate with a shop provides contrast.

SECTION F

WOLVERTON:
Now absorbed into Milton Keynes, Wolverton is Anglo-Saxon in origin but its main claim to individual fame is as a Victorian construction centre for rolling stock, with the great Queen herself opening the station here in 1845. The area includes Old Wolverton and Wolverton Mill with the newer part consisting mainly of Victorian terraces.

HISTORY

Until very recently, the villages along this stretch generally earned their living from the land, with many being parts of much larger estates. As was often the case in such economies, life was hard and incomes were often supplemented with other trades, usually carried out in the winter or by the women, such as lace making, which thrived in Ashton and Hanslope.

Many of these villages feature in the Domesday Book, with a good proportion being able to trace their routes back to Saxon, if not Roman, times. Hanslope, for example, has claim to Roman origins through the discovery of coins from that period. The A5 – the Roman Watling Street – passes to the south of the section and Stony Stratford was also the site of some Roman fortresses.

The River Ouse was a boundary for Danelaw, the area administered by the Vikings, and many of the local churches can date themselves back to Saxon times, even if the buildings themselves are usually later. Haversham, for example, means 'Haefer's Homestead' in Saxon. As elsewhere, the Norman invasion had a marked impact on the area, with the imposition of a feudal regime. At the time of the invasion Hanslope was owned by Aldene, one of Harold's bodyguards, and he was duly replaced by Winemar the Fleming.

The influence of the church was less strong, although Bradwell had its own Benedictine Priory, Bradwell Abbey, and Shutlanger to the west of Stoke Bruerne had its own monastery. Bradwell was founded in 1155 and survived for 300 years, but unlike many other such institutions, failed to accumulate much wealth and was more famous for its piety than its grandeur. A small chapel is all that remains of Bradwell today. Likewise, a chapel remains at Shutlanger, although this is now used as a children's nursery.

In time, the area covered in this section became well populated with castles as the local lords attempted to protect their possessions in lands that were quite distant from the main seats of power. Alderton, Haversham, Wolverton and Castlethorpe all had their own fortifications, with the latter

> Whisper it quietly, but Hanslope Park, once the local manor house, is home to the Government's Communications Centre and is rumoured to be the place where the Technical Security Department of MI6 operates.

owing its very existence to the castle, as its name suggests, the 'thorpe' in its title meaning village.

As the monarchy became more established, this castle, like all the others hereabouts, disappeared. The castle's owner, William Mauduit, was in constant dispute with King John and even led a rebellion against him at one point, but he was ultimately to lose his castle. These days all that remains of the motte and bailey construction is preserved as a scheduled ancient monument. Things turned out well for the Mauduits, as later on they succeeded to the Earldom of Warwick. Hanslope was eventually given to Princess Elizabeth, later to be queen.

As time went on, kings began to favour the area, with Grafton even earning the suffix 'Regis' when Elizabeth's father, Henry VIII, stayed at the Manor. Prior to this visit, Grafton had an even greater role in royal history when Henry's grandfather, Edward IV, married Elizabeth Woodville there in private on May Day 1464. Elizabeth was the daughter of a local squire and went on to become the mother of the famous 'Princes in the Tower', who were last seen alive in public at the Rose and Crown in Stony Stratford.

Although Grafton had a brief involvement in the Civil War, the centuries that followed the Tudors tended to be uneventful around these parts. Occasionally, new large houses were built, such as Stoke Park Pavillions south of Stoke Bruerne, built by Inigo Jones in the 1630s, but these were the exception rather than the rule.

> Stoke Park Pavillions was built for Sir Francis Crane, who introduced tapestry making into England. In its time it was regarded as one of the finest examples of Palladian architecture.

Stony Stratford grew to some prominence due to its position on the great coaching routes, and in the early 1800s as many as 200 coaches a day stopped here, but this trade ended abruptly when the railway came. With its long High Street, Stony Stratford, separate to all the towns absorbed by Milton Keynes, retains some sense of independence, although two massive conflagrations in 1736 and 1742 restricted its growth.

The arrival of the Victorian era, notably the impact of first the canals and then the railways, were the next major events along this section. Old Stratford used to have the Buckingham Arm of the Grand Union run through it, and many other villages along this section such as Cosgrove and Stoke Bruerne were also beneficiaries of the new transport system.

> Housing in New Bradwell lined the top of the hill, which meant that supplies of water on Mondays (wash day) would regularly become interrupted when local steam trains took on water there from the newly built water column, leading to angry scenes between local women and engine drivers.

The railways were equally significant, nowhere more so than around New Bradwell and Wolverton. New Bradwell was a 'new village', that later became absorbed into the 'new town' (and subsequently city) of Milton Keynes. It swallowed up nearby Stantonbury, a parish of a dozen houses, in 1857, and grew at such a pace that within three years it needed its own church and school.

New Bradwell was one of two stops on a branch off the London–Birmingham railway, the other being Great Linford. Housing grew up around the station and rows of Victorian railwaymen's cottages are still the predominant architectural style there today.

Wolverton was originally an Anglo-Saxon village (the name means 'Wulfhere's estate') with its own motte and bailey castle as well as a medieval village, the mounds of which are still visible today from the towpath. The remains of the original Saxon church are incorporated into the church of the Holy Trinity in Old Wolverton.

Wolverton initially grew from these origins as a result of the canal, but moved half a mile north when the railway arrived in 1838. The site of the old

Wolverton Wharf is now occupied by the Galleon pub. Wolverton's fate was changed forever when it was chosen to become the locomotive repair shop for the London and Birmingham Railway. Locomotives were built here for the next thirty years, and also repaired until the site focussed on carriages over a decade later. Wolverton was also home to the Royal Train.

Since the passing of the railway age, the dominant influence, in the south of the section at least, has been the rapid rise of Milton Keynes and the development of some of the local villages into suburbs or dormitories of the new city. Ideally placed midway between Birmingham and London, and just off the M1 motorway, Milton Keynes was originally planned to take 40,000. This grew rapidly to 100,000 and is now moving towards the 200,000 mark.

Wolverton and the Stratfords maintain a semblance of independence from their large southern neighbour, but are to all intents and purposes part of it. Other places such as Roade have also felt the effect, this village doubling in size in the middle period of the second half of the twentieth century. The new city's influence is largely a benign one, however, and comes upon you suddenly, with the aqueduct over the Great Ouse acting as a physical boundary between the city itself and sleepy Northamptonshire.

THE NATURAL LANDSCAPE

While unprepossessing to look at, the River Tove is one of the dominant natural features along this stretch, with the Ouse, which it joins just east of Cosgrove, making a late bid for recognition. Upper Lias Clay forms the main soil along most of the southern part of the section, with the rivers providing alluvial soil and gravel terraces. Large lakes continue the water theme north of Milton Kenyes.

The pattern of large, open and very flat fields established earlier, continues, and hills remain rare features, as the relative lack of locks confirms. Alderton, Ashton and Grafton Regis sit slightly proud of the landscape, although only the latter is noticeable from the towpath. Once again, woodland is noticeable only by its absence.

ACCESS AND TRANSPORT

ROADS
The A5 makes a brief appearance in the south of the section, but the main trunk road is the A508 which spurs off the A5 at Old Stratford and follows a route east of the canal, taking in Yardley Gobion and Grafton Regis before crossing over the water south of Stoke Bruerne and passing through Roade. Otherwise, a network of minor roads links the villages together while the M1 passes largely unnoticed across the top of the section.

RAIL
The railway echoes the route of the canal, but to its east, although the only station is Wolverton. This sits on the main Euston–Birmingham line with the next stop south Milton Keynes.

Train operators serving this area are:

- Silverlink (08457 818 919)
- Virgin Trains (08457 222333)

Otherwise, National Train Enquiries can be reached on 08457 484950.

BUSES

The following list sets out the main buses along this section although it is advisable to check before using them as some buses only run on certain days and others may have been withdrawn since publication of this Guide. It is also worth checking for more local services, in particular those linking districts of Milton Keynes where there are a number of circular and school-term-time only services.

- 4E – *linking Wolverton and Stony Stratford with Milton Kenyes (MKM)*
- 5 – *Hartwell to Bletchley via Hanslope, Castlethorpe, Wolverton, Milton Keynes (MKM)*
- 12 – *Stony Stratford, Wolverton and Milton Keynes (Open University) (MKM)*
- 14/14a – *linking Old and New Stratford with Milton Keynes (MKM)*
- 23/30/31 – *Stony Stratford, Wolverton, Milton Keynes (MKM)*
- 33 – *Northampton to Milton Keynes via Roade, Hartwell, Hanslope, Castlethorpe, Wolverton (UC)*
- 86 – *Stoke Bruerne to Northampton (MKM)*
- 87 – *Shutlanger, Stoke Bruerne, Ashton, Roade, Northampton (UC)*
- 89 – *Northampton to Milton Keynes via Yardley Gobion, Cosgrove, Old Stratford, Stony Stratford (UC)*
- X4 – *Milton Keynes to Peterborough via Roade (UC)*

Contact details for bus operators in this area are listed below, although Traveline (www.traveline.org.uk) on 0870 6082608 can give details of specific services between 7 a.m. and 10 p.m.:

- MK Metro, Milton Keynes (01908 668366)
- UC – United Counties, Northampton (01604 601502)

TAXIS

The following list gives a selection of the taxi operators in this section:

- ABC 3 Counties, Stoke Bruerne (01604 864884)
- Bill's Taxis, New Bradwell (07885 577876)
- Buckingham Cars, Hanslope (01908 510510)
- Carlton Car Service, Cosgrove (01908 307030)
- On Time Cars, Stoke Bruerne (01604 864727)
- Speedline, Old Stratford (01908 260260)
- United Cars, Wolverton (01908 222444)

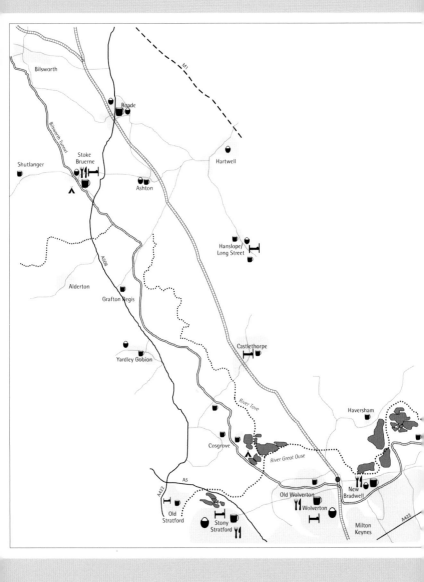

Key

══════ Canal	🔵 Built up area
·········· River	🔴 Stations
⊞⊞⊞⊞⊞ Railway	🟢 Open water
─ ─ ─ Motorway	
──── A Road	
──── B Road	

🍵 Shops

⊢ Accomodation

△ Campsite

☕ Pub

🍴 Restaurant

Bilsworth

Roade

Stoke Bruerne

Shutlanger

Ashton

Hartwell

Hanslope/
Long Street

Alderton

Grafton Regis

Yardley Gobion

Castlethorpe

Haversham

River Tove

Cosgrove

River Great Ouse

Old Stratford

Old Wolverton

New Bradwell

Stony Stratford

Wolverton

Milton Keynes

Bilsworth Tunnel

A508

A5

A422

A422

M1

BASICS

INTRODUCTION

Sitting between Northampton and Milton Keynes, many of the villages along this stretch have carved out a niche as small communities, often with their own pub and, if they are lucky, a shop. Just off the main road, Stoke Bruerne has a 'preserved' air about it but is none the worse for it, while places such as Hanslope and Grafton Regis remain distinctly separate before the presence of Milton Keynes makes itself felt as the section draws to a close.

As the canal passes to the east and closer to the centre of Milton Keynes after leaving this section, the city is covered in detail in the companion Tempus Towpath Guide, *The Grand Union Canal (South)*.

SHOPPING

Stony Stratford and Wolverton are the main shopping destinations along this stretch, although many of the villages along the way have their own village store or, occasionally, one of the branded mini-supermarkets. Stoke Bruerne, Hartwell and Old Stratford are all good examples of the former, while the Bridge Stores at Old Stratford are convenient for the towpath.

There is a Costcutter at one of the petrol stations in Roade, as well as a basic off-licence at another, and a newsagent and pharmacy in the older part of the village. There is also a Costcutter in the housing estate in Yardley Gobion and a Co-op at New Bradwell, easily missed just off the towpath at Bridge 72, where there is also an off-licence and a fish bar.

Hanslope and Ashton are the best places to head if you want something a bit more back to basics, with the former having a butcher who also sells fruit and vegetables (as well as a tiny newsagent and a Londis), while The Vale Farmhouse Shop at Ashton is open Thursday, Friday and Saturday (07711 628246), with an emphasis on Italian foodstuffs and home-reared meat.

Stony Stratford has a long High Street with a good range of shops and banks, including a number of specialists. The shops continue along the Wolverton Road and there are three small arcades: Swinfen's Yard, Stratford Arcade and Timor Court, which are worth popping into to see what you can find.

Wolverton has a large Tesco a short trek from the towpath as well as a Netto, along with a long row of High Street shops running parallel with the railway line, including a useful hardware store.

EATING AND DRINKING

Most of the villages along this stretch have their own pubs (with one or two exceptions), while Stony Stratford's past as a coaching stop has left a legacy of watering holes.

SECTION F

The sign at Castlethorpe.

PUBS

- The Cock, Roade (01604 862544)
- The George Inn, Roade (01604 862500)
- The Boat Inn, Stoke Bruerne (01604 862428)
- The Navigation, Stoke Bruerne (01604 864988) – *family pub with children's play equipment outside*
- The Plough Inn, Shutlanger (01604 862327) – *specialises in fish*
- The Old Crown, Ashton (01604 862268)
- The Cock Inn, Hanslope (01908 510553)
- The Watts Arms, Hanslope (01908 510246)
- The Globe Inn, Long Street (01908 510336)
- The White Hart, Grafton Regis (01908 542123)
- The Coffee Pot, Yardley Gobion (01908 542106) – *complete with skittles alley*
- The Carrington Arms, Castlethorpe (01908 510257)
- The Barley Mow, Cosgrove (01908 562957) – *canalside pub, Cosgrove*
- The Navigation, Cosgrove (01908 543156)
- The Greyhound, Haversham (01908 313487)
- The Galleon, Old Wolverton (01908 313176) – *by Bridge 68*
- The County Arms, New Bradwell (01908 313840)
- Cuba, New Bradwell (01908 313904)
- The Forresters Arms, New Bradwell (01908 312348)
- The New Inn, New Bradwell (01908 312094) – *canalside*
- Crauford Arms, Wolverton (01908 313864)
- The North Western, Wolverton (01908 312200)
- The Swan, Old Stratford (01908 563654)
- The Bull Hotel, Stony Stratford (01908 567104)
- The Duke of Wellington, Stony Stratford (01908 563383)
- The Forresters Arms, Stony Stratford (01908 567115)
- The Fox and Hounds, Stony Stratford (01908 563307)
- The Plough, Stony Stratford (01908 561936)
- The White Horse, Stony Stratford (01908 567082)
- The Proud Perch, Great Linford (01908 398461)

EATING

Stony Stratford is the place to head for if you are looking for a good range of restaurants. The town's coaching past has attracted a number of establishments offering a range of cuisines from Japanese to Greek, with the usual Indian, Chinese, Thai and English thrown in. Stoke Bruerne is also worth a visit, as are many of the pubs along this section.

- Al'Tamborista, Stony Stratford (01908 262632) – *Italian*
- Bekash, Stony Stratford (01908 562249) – *Indian*
- Bruernes Lock, Stoke Bruerne (01604 863654) – *a là carte restaurant*
- Calverton Lodge, Stony Stratford (01908 261241) – *English*
- Eastern Paradise, Wolverton (01908 312969) – *Indian*
- First Class Restaurant, Stony Stratford (01908 307688) – *Japanese*
- The Golden Sea, Stony Stratford (01908 562185) – *Chinese*
- The Greek Villager, Wolverton (01908 221324) – *Greek*
- Indigo, Stony Stratford (01908 263872) – *Indian*
- Julia Bistro, Stony Stratford (01908 262320) – *English*
- The Malaysian Restaurant, Stony Stratford (01908 260026)
- Moghul Palace, Stony Stratford (01908 566577) – *Indian*
- New Bradwell Tandoori, New Bradwell (01908 316664) – *Indian*
- Passage to India, Stony Stratford (01908 567610) – *Indian*
- Peking Restaurant, Stony Stratford (01908 563120) – *Chinese*
- The Raj Dynasty, New Bradwell (01908 225599) – *Indian*
- Roosters, Stony Stratford (01908 569353) – *Greek*
- Royal Thai, Stony Stratford (01908 565338) – *Thai*
- Stables Wine Bar, Stony Stratford (01908 561102) – *Mexican*

Stoke Bruerne and Stony Stratford are also the best places for light snacks, with a choice of places to go:

- Kay's Kitchen, Stony Stratford (01908 265551)
- The Old Chapel, Stoke Bruerne (01604 863284)
- MacIntyre's, Stony Stratford (01908 568267)
- Mangetout, Stony Stratford (01908 265551)
- Muffins Coffee Shop, Stony Stratford (01908 262320)

The canal near Grafton Regis.

Boat weighing scales at Stoke Bruerne.

SLEEPING

There are plenty of places to stay along this stretch, with a wide choice of bed and breakfasts making up for the relatively thin choice of hotels. For some reason, the Hanslope/Castlethorpe area is particularly rich in bed and breakfasts and inns, with a number of working farms also available to stay at.

> The Cock and Bull pubs in Stony Stratford are thought to have started the phrase 'cock and bull story'. At both coaching inns, gossip would be exchanged and magnified until it became barely believable.

HOTELS

- Bull Hotel, Stony Stratford (01908 567104)
- The Cock Hotel, Stony Stratford (01908 567733)
- The Different Drummer Hotel, Stony Stratford (01908 564733)
- The Hatton Court Hotel, Hanslope (01908 510044)

- The Old George Hotel, Stony Stratford (01908 562181) – *restaurant and free house*
- Roade House Hotel, Roade (01604 863372)
- The Roman Rooms, Wolverton (01908 318020)
- Travelodge Milton Keynes, Old Stratford (0870 0850950)

BED AND BREAKFAST/GUEST HOUSES

- 3 Rookery Barns, Stoke Bruerne (01604 862274) – *barn conversion B&B*
- 36 Oxford Street, Wolverton (01908 313618)
- 110 Clarence Road, Stony Stratford (01908 562381)
- Balney Grounds, Castlethorpe (01908 510208)
- Beam End Stoke Park, Stoke Bruerne (01604 864802)
- Crauford Arms, Wolverton (01908 313864)
- Chantry Farm, Hanslope (01908 510269)
- Cuckoo Hill Farm, Hanslope (01908 510748)
- Fegans View, Stony Stratford (01908 562128)
- Ikoyi Guest House, Old Stratford (01908 563114)
- Leamington Farm, Castlethorpe (01908 510235) – *working farm*
- Lincoln Lodge Farm, Castlethorpe (01908 510152) – *working farm*
- Manor House Farm, Castlethorpe (01908 510216) – *working farm*
- Milford Leys, Castlethorpe (01908 510153)
- Spinney Lodge Farm, Hanslope (01908 510267)
- Stonehouse B&B, Stoke Bruerne (01604 864011)
- Telford House B&B, Stony Stratford (01908 564206)
- Waterways Cottage, Stoke Bruerne (01604 863865)
- The Watts Arms, Hanslope (01908 510246)
- The White Horse, Stony Stratford (01908 567082)
- Woad Farm, Hanslope (01908 510985)

CAMPING

Cosgrove Leisure Park (01908 563360) is one of the largest inland camping sites in the country, situated on the Northants/Bucks border next to the River Tove with 500 hook-up points. If you like your camping a little less crowded, there is also Home Farm in Stoke Bruerne (01604 863598), although this is open to Caravan Club members only. There is also a youth hostel at Bradwell (01908 310944) situated in an old seventeenth-century farmhouse.

Stoke Bruerne's old tramway celebrated in sculpture.

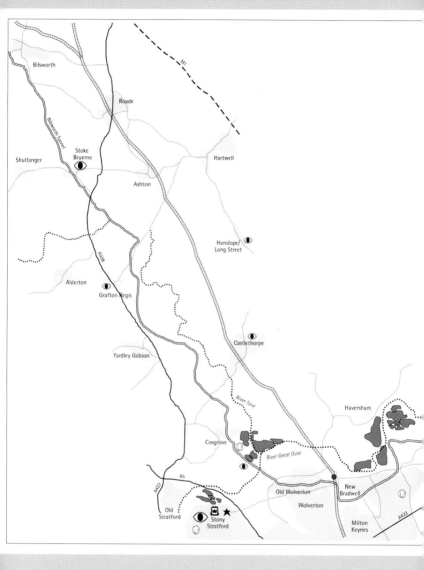

Key

═══	Canal
··········	River
▥▥▥▥	Railway
— — —	Motorway
———	A Road
———	B Road

🟤 (built up area)	Built up area
🔴	Stations
🔵	Open water

◉	Site/Sight
◎	Leisure
★	Entertainment
🖼	Culture

SEEING AND DOING

INTRODUCTION

This section is bookended with two significant canal features: the Stoke Bruerne Museum and the flight of locks just after it, and the aqueduct over the River Ouse that marks the approach to the north of Milton Keynes. In between, the villages scattered about the section offer up illustrations of their past, although few of these have really stood the test of time.

SIGHTS

Alone along this section, Stoke Bruerne can claim to be a canal village, something it turns to its advantage without any embarrassment. Pubs and places to eat cluster around the top lock and, even before you reach the museum, there is usually plenty of evidence of the way the village likes to keep the canal 'alive' in the form of school parties or restored boats.

The museum itself (01604 864199) is located in a restored corn mill right by the water's edge and, like its counterparts elsewhere, tells the story of the canals – how they were built, how people lived on them and the difference they made to the areas they cut through. There is also an excellent shop with a particularly fine collection of books for sale. The boat-weighing scales by the top lock were originally on the Glamorganshire Canal.

> NB Indian Chief offers canal trips for up to forty people, including trips through the tunnel and the locks (01604 862428).

Stoke Bruerne has the added advantage of sitting on the southern portal of the Blisworth Tunnel and day-boating can be arranged from the Stoke Bruerne Boat Co. (01604 862428) if you feel like investigating the tunnel's wet interior.

> The horse-drawn tramway at Stoke Breurne was a stop-gap measure constructed to carry goods over the yet to be completed Blisworth Tunnel.

Head up towards the portal and you may just pick up the route of the old tramway above the towpath. This is marked out by some wire sculptures and claims to be Northamptonshire's first railway.

Like many of the villages along this stretch, Stoke Bruerne also has a fine church, parts of which date back to the twelfth century, although it is mainly fourteenth and fifteenth century with a vestry built in 1881. Outside the village stands Stoke Park, where it is possible to see the Palladian pavilions from the now long-gone house. Also outside the village is the Rookery Open Farm (01604 864855), open March to November, but closed Tuesdays.

Hanslope is worth a detour, sitting as it does somewhat proud of the surrounding landscape and offering a good sense of what life might have been like in one of these small rural villages. There is a wide marketplace and an impressive run of thatched cottages known as Horseshoe Cottages, so called because they form an arc.

The church here is also worth a look. Dedicated to St James the Great, it has a 186ft-high castellated fifteenth-century tower which is a landmark for some distance when walking the towpath. The oldest part of the church dates back to 1160, although there was a church prior to this date outside the village.

Look out for the funeral banners in St James' church; these used to be hung outside the front door of the house of the deceased for a year.

Some of the original stone corbels survive in the roof, with two of them playing musical instruments, one a horn and the other a mandore, a plucked instrument similar to a lute, popular in the twelfth and thirteenth centuries. Although impressive, the spire used to be taller, a lightning strike in 1805 reducing it to its base. It was rebuilt, but lost 20ft along the way. Thankfully, its crocketed style, with pinnacles and flying buttresses, was maintained.

See 'Learn More and Links' for details on how to access an impressive village trail compiled by the local school children in Hanslope in 1999. This includes features such as the grand Vicarage Court, now flats but at one time a palatial home for the local priest, the local newsagents (once the telephone exchange) and signs of the seven pubs that once watered the village.

Although only small today, in Norman times Alderton had its own castle, the site of which was recently bought for £20,000, complete with moat and mound. The new owner invited Channel 4's *Time Team* to investigate and they managed to reconstruct a picture of the castle in its heyday.

Grafton's place in history has been explored in the 'Shapers' section and if you were thinking that appreciation of that history requires a lot of imagination, then you are in luck. Local guides are available (01908 542211) and, if you can get a group together, they will conduct you through a tour of the village dressed in period costume, telling tales through from medieval to modern times.

Little remains of Castlethorpe's Norman castle, but the village is an attractive one with unusual eighteenth-century buildings built of cream-coloured limestone, and the village has good views out over the Tove Valley.

It is at Cosgrove that the towpath comes across the Great Ouse Aqueduct. This is the second aqueduct to stand here; the first, built of brick, lasted only three years, damming up the river below when it collapsed. It was replaced by the present cast-iron construction in 1881.

New Bradwell sits on the canal and has the distinction of having a windmill, built in 1817, which, with a certain symmetry, continued to function until 1871. This has now been restored and runs off an electric motor.

Look out below the aqueduct to see if you can pick out the old line of the canal and the locks that used to take it down to the river. It sits in a copse to the west of the canal and south of the river. The current Cosgrove Lock was part of the run.

Stony Stratford is a good example of an eighteenth-century coaching town, although most of its older history has been destroyed by a combination of fire and the activities of man. A good example is the Eleanor Cross that once stood here, which was a victim of the Civil War. New Bradwell and Wolverton bring us a little closer to modern times with their strong railway antecedents, while Milton Keynes to the south is the very epitome of what twentieth-century man can achieve and is covered in detail in the Tempus Towpath Guide *The Grand Union Canal (South)*.

CULTURE AND ENTERTAINMENT

The main focus of sporting activity in this section is undoubtedly Cosgrove Leisure Park (01908 563360), which has not only a large watersports area with windsurfing and jet-skiing, but also a decent mini-golf course. The park is also a large caravan and fishing centre.

> The stand at the football ground in Wolverton, built in 1899, has claims to being the first in England, although at the time of writing it was due to be demolished in favour of an apartment block.

This section is a little thin on the ground when it comes to formal leisure centres, although Stantonbury Campus (01908 324466) has a complex of wet and dry facilities including a six-lane swimming pool and a fitness studio, while the Watling Way Centre in Stony Stratford (01908 562257) has an indoor pool and a sports hall. Both of these are probably best described as useful for those seeking fitness rather than pure fun. Less serious is the complex of three open-air swimming pools in Wolverton (01908 322200), open May to September, weather permitting.

> On 2 June 1830 Hanslope was the venue for the prizefighting championship of Great Britain, the site chosen as it was close to county borders, making it difficult for the local constabulary to stop it. The contest ended after 47 rounds when the challenger, a Scot called Sandy M'Kay, collapsed and later died. He is buried in the local graveyard.

The main focus of cultural life in this section is probably Stony Live!, a festival which began in 1998. This attracts musicians from around the South Midlands and East Anglia to the town for a week in June, maintaining the town's reputation as a focus for live music, which is also encapsulated by its 'Folk on the Green' live (and free!) folk festival.

Places with a strong tradition of live music include the Fox and Hounds pub, Cock Hotel and the Vaults wine bar, although those seeking nightclubs are probably best advised to head south into Milton Keynes where there is an embarrassment of choice.

Look out for ducks by Bridge 60.

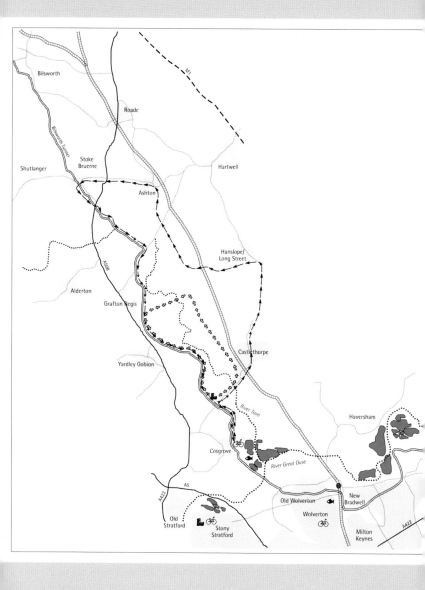

Bilsworth

Roade

M1

Bilsworth Tunnel

Stoke
Bruerne

Shutlanger

Hartwell

Ashton

Alderton

Hanslope/
Long Street

A508

Grafton Regis

Yardley Gobion

Castlethorpe

River Tove

Cosgrove

Haversham

River Great Ouse

A422

A5

Old
Stratford

Stony
Stratford

Old Wolverton

Wolverton

New
Bradwell

Milton
Keynes

A422

Key

▬▬▬	Canal	
·········	River	
▥▥▥▥	Railway	
▬ ▬ ▬	Motorway	
▬▬▬	A Road	
▬▬▬	B Road	

⬤	Built up area	
⬤	Stations	
⬤	Open water	

🚲➤	Cycling route/outlet
👢⇨	Walking route/outlet
🐟	Fishing spot/outlet
⚑	Golf course/outlet
∩	Riding outlet

SAMPLING

INTRODUCTION

This is an easy section to sample away from the towpath, with a network of paths and a number of minor roads. Quiet for long stretches, the section ends with the stunning Great Ouse Aqueduct with its excellent views out over the valley below, before steadily building up into the more urbanised areas to the north of Milton Keynes.

The section is covered by OS Explorer Map 207, Newport Pagnell and Northampton South.

WALKING

This section of the canal is peppered with formal walking routes as well as other places to head off into. The Grafton Way joins west of Yardley Gobion and goes through Cosgrove and along the aqueduct before linking up with the North Buckinghamshire Way. There is also the Milton Keynes Boundary Walk which passes down north of Hanslope before joining the towpath at Bridge 58. It then follows the line of the canal before heading south after also passing over the aqueduct, following the route of the Great Ouse.

The Hanslope circular ride, although designed primarily for horses, does what its name suggests, passing through Castlethorpe to the south and over the motorway to the east. The Midshires Way comes in through the north of the section and ends south-east of Roade.

Yardley Gobion and Stoke Bruerne act as particular magnets for local footpaths. Salcey Forest lies north-east of Hartwell and is known for its 'druids' or veteran oaks, some of which are thought to be over 500 years old.

> Look out for the rare Black Poplars at Castlethorpe Mill which offer up a display of scarlet catkins in spring, followed by bright green young leaves. The rough bark and burred trunks of these trees add to their distinctiveness.

The Great Ouse has its own park and can be followed from New Bradwell, over the top of Wolverton and under the aqueduct before passing to the west of Stony Stratford. The River Tove can be followed from north of Cosgrove but gets trickier north of Castlethorpe, after which it is best admired from a distance, something Walk F allows you to do.

Along the footpath to Alderton from Stoke Bruerne is a nature reserve established on the site of an old brickworks built by the canal company to allow them to build their locks and bridges. Particularly worthy of note here are the reed beds and rough grassland, with the latter providing a feeding ground for barn owls.

Grafton Regis Meadow, on the road between Grafton Regis and Ashton, is one of the last remaining hay meadows in the county. Being protected from ploughing has led to a diversity of flora including cuckooflower, great burnet and southern marsh-orchid. Look out also for curlew, moorhens and herons.

Likewise, Mill Crook, near the junction of the Hanslope Circular Ride and the Milton Keynes Boundary Walk, is another traditional hay meadow with over fifty species of flowering plant and twenty species of grass.

SECTION F WALK
Along the Tove Valley

Description:	*A flat walk along towpath and bridleway*
Distance:	*6 miles*
Duration:	*2.5 hours*
Starting point:	*Grid Reference 787437, OS Explorer 207 (E)*
Nearest refreshment:	*The Navigation, Thrupp Wharf*

Start at the pub and head north towards Castlethorpe, ignoring the footpath to your right immediately after the canal, and another immediately after the river. Head slightly uphill until houses begin to appear on your left and pick up the bridleway on your left on Station Road. A sign will direct you towards Milford Leys and Lincoln Lodge. This bridleway is easy to follow and flat all the way, and constitutes part of the Hanslope Circular Ride. There are plentiful views down to the left towards the river and over the valley towards the canal, while Hanslope's church spire behind you remains a talisman for much of the route.

Continue on the bridleway for 2.5 miles until you meet a cross-roads of paths where you should head left, picking up part of the Milton Keynes Boundary Walk. This takes you back down to the canal, crossing the river along the way. The canal is reached via Bridge 58, with the towpath lying on the valley side. Head left and follow the path back to your starting point via Yardley Wharf.

Walking equipment outlets along this section include:
• The Outdoor Shop, Stony Stratford (01908 568913)

CYCLING

Sustrans National Cycleway Route passes through Castlethorpe on the Hanslope Road on its way into Milton Keynes, and there are a number of minor roads in the area north-east of the A508 which offer a relatively traffic-free environment to enjoy parts of this section by road.

To sample this section on two wheels is to start in Cosgrove and head north on the towpath as far as Bridge 64, where you pick up the road to the right heading into Castlethorpe. At the T-junction head north to Hanslope, and then head north-west to Long Street. Pick up the road on the left before the pub and follow the road downhill, including the sharp bend left at Pindon End, all the way into Ashton. Turn left at the junction and then left again, down to the A508. Dog-leg over to the right into Stoke Bruerne, where you pick up the towpath again and head back to your starting point – a total of around 16 miles.

Cycle outlets along this section include:

• The Cycle King, Stony Stratford (01908 566722)	• Grafton Cycle Co., Wolverton (01908 282121)

RIDING

Formal riding routes along this section include Swan's Way, a long-distance path linking the Salcey Forest and Goring on Thames via Haversham, which is identifiable by its signs showing a swan within a horseshoe on a green directional arrow, which links with the Three Shires Way near Hanslope.

Hanslope itself has the Hanslope Circular Ride as well as sections of bridleway heading north-east from Stocking Green Farm and from Newport Road. More bridleway heads west from the road to Castlethorpe which runs west from the A508 between Grafton Regis and Yardley Gobion.

Horse-riding establishments and outlets along this section include:

- Ashton Stables, Ashton (01604 864557)
- Bryline Riding Surfaces, Roade (01604 864227)
- Malt Mill Farm, Castlethorpe Road, Hanslope (01908 511329) – *home of*

  the Milton Keynes Eventing Centre, with stabling for over fifty horses and over 140 acres of open fields
- Wharf Line Stables, Yardley Gobion (07932 625813)

FISHING

The main angling club along this section is the Northampton Nene AC (01604 705205) which controls the canal between Bridges 56 and 62. Bream up to 6lb can be caught near the beginning of this run, with carp to 20lb between Bridges 61 and 62.

The Britannia AC (01604 470190) controls the section from Bridge 62 and 64 where there is good bream, carp, tench and perch, while the Galleon AC (01908 669638) operates the section from south of the aqueduct over the Great Ouse to the smaller one at New Bradwell, with the Milton Keynes AA (01908 691777) picking up responsibility from here on in.

Milton Keynes AA also controls lake fishing at Wolverton Mill (good for carp) and Bradwell Lake (good for pike and tench), and sections of the Ouse and Tove.

Cosgrove Leisure Park has twelve lakes and two rivers to fish, as well as the canal nearby, and also a tackle shop. The lakes are stocked with carp up to 25lb, bream up to 11lb, roach and rudd up to 2lb, tench up to 10lb, perch to over 4lb and there are also pike running up to 35lb. The Great Ouse and the Tove both have good stocks of chub, roach and dace, with some river carp, pike and perch.

Outlets selling fishing supplies along this stretch include:

- Great Linford Angling Centre, Wolverton (0870 6092390)
- Lakeside Stores, Cosgrove Leisure

  Park (01908 563360)
- Sportsmans Lodge, Wolverton (01908 313158)

OTHER

Those contemplating a quick round of golf as a way of sampling this section will be disappointed; the closest they will get is the mini golf at Cosgrove Leisure Park.

Learn More And Links

For those wishing to delve a little further into the places and events covered in this guide the following list, while far from comprehensive, should act as a useful starting point:

TOURIST INFORMATION
- Birmingham, The Rotunda (0870 428 1859)
- Warwick, Jury Street (01926 492212)
- Leamington Spa, Royal Pump Rooms (01926 742762)

WEBSITES OFFERING INFORMATION ON SPECIFIC PLACES OR EVENTS:
- www.solihull.gov.uk – *local government site covering Solihull*
- www.solihull-online.com – *more on Solihull*
- www.solihullparish.org.uk – *for more on St Alphege's church*
- www.aboutb93.com – *site covering Knowle and Dorridge*
- www.aghs.virtualbrum.co.uk – *Acocks Green website*
- www.birminghamuk.com/historicbirmingham.htm – *Birmingham history*
- www.royal-leamington-spa.co.uk – *Leamington Spa portal*
- www.whitnashtowncouncil.gov.uk – *more on Whitnash*
- www.warwick-uk.co.uk – *more on Warwick*
- www.otba.org.uk – *site covering Leamington Old Town*
- www.braunston.net – *village website*
- www.daventrytowncouncil.gov.uk – *more on Daventry with history section*
- www.longbuckby.net – *village site for Long Buckby*
- www.blisworth.org.uk – *village site for Blisworth, with photos*
- www.northamptonshiresearch.com – *portal for all things to do with Northamptonshire*
- www.ashtonvillage.co.uk – *village site for Ashton*
- www.mkheritage.co.uk/hghs/index.html - *Hanslope history and village trail*
- www.grafton-regis.co.uk – *village site for Grafton Regis*
- www.mkheritage.co.uk/osrg – *site looking at Old Stratford*
- www.stonystratford.co.uk – *site on Stony Stratford*
- www.mkheritage.co.uk/hdhs/index.html - *more on Hanslope*
- www.mkheritage.co.uk/mkm/stonystratford – *site on Stony Stratford*
- www.mkheritage.co.uk – *much on the villages surrounding Milton Keynes*
- www.miltonkeynes.com/info/village_info - *more on Milton Keynes villages*
- www.mkweb – *portal for all things to do with Milton Keynes*

LOCALLY PRODUCED FOOD:
- www.bigbarn.co.uk – *the UK's main site for locally produced food*

BOOKS OFFERING FURTHER DETAIL ON SPECIFIC PLACES
OR ASPECTS OF LOCAL HISTORY:

- *Solihull Past*, Sue Bates (Phillimore 2001)
- *Around Knowle and Dorridge*, Charles Lines (Alan Sutton Publishing 1996)
- *James Brindley: The First Canal Builder*, Nick Corble (Tempus Publishing 2005)
- *Grafton Regis: The History of a Northamptonshire Village*, Charles FitzRoy and Keith Harry (eds) (Merton Priory Press 2000)

TRANSPORT:

- www.mkweb.co.uk/transport – *for details of bus and other routes in the Milton Keynes area*
- Sustrans Information Service, PO Box 21, Bristol BS99 2HA (0117 929 0888) www.sustrans.org.uk
- Central Trains www.centraltrains.co.uk
- Chiltern Railways www.chilternrailways.co.uk
- Silverlink www.silverlink-trains.com
- Virgin Trains www.virgintrains.co.uk

OTHER:

- www.nationaltrust.org.uk – *website for the National Trust, useful in particular for more on the properties mentioned in the Guide*
- www.ramblers.org.uk – *for more on walking routes covered in this Guide*
- The British Horse Society, Stoneleigh Deer Park, Kenilworth, Warks CV8 2XZ (08701 202244)

INDEX

Tempus is keen to keep these guides as up to date as possible. If you have any suggestions for inclusion in the next edition of this guide, or would like to point out any changes since it was written, please email us at towpathguides@tempus-publishing.com